CANYON NATIONAL
PARKS

Welcome to Zion and Bryce Canyon National Parks

Zion and Bryce Canyon are well known for their hoodoos, slot canyons, and other red-rock formations. But different landscapes also await, from hanging gardens to emerald pools. There's plenty of history, too—ruins, petroglyphs, pioneer graffiti, and ghost towns memorialize what once was. This book was produced during the COVID-19 pandemic. As you plan your trip to Zion and Bryce Canyon National Parks, please confirm that places are still open and let us know when we need to make updates by writing to us at editors@fodors.com.

TOP REASONS TO GO

★ **Hiking:** Trails meander beside rivers, through woods, along or under canyon rims, and amid hoodoos.

★ **Family Fun:** Park programs and outdoor adventures make family vacations a pleasure.

★ **Scenic Drives:** Routes traverse scenery that takes in snowcapped mountains as well as colorful desert.

★ **Stargazing:** Clear skies make astronomy a highlight throughout the region.

★ **R&R Aplenty:** Careen down a mountain (by bike or on skis); hit the greens; unwind in a spa; dine with a view.

Contents

1 **EXPERIENCE ZION AND BRYCE CANYON NATIONAL PARKS....7**

15 Ultimate Experiences............... 8

What's Where 14

Birds, Reptiles, and Mammals of Zion and Bryce Canyon 16

Plants of Zion and Bryce Canyon.......... 18

Best Trails of Zion and Bryce Canyon 20

Welcome to Zion and Bryce Canyon 22

Zion and Bryce Canyon with Kids.... 25

What to Watch and Read.................. 26

2 **TRAVEL SMART......27**

Know Before You Go 28

Getting Here and Around.............. 30

Essentials.................. 34

On the Calendar...... 44

Contacts.................... 47

3 **ZION NATIONAL PARK** 49

Welcome to Zion National Park 50

Planning 54

Zion Canyon.............. 59

Kolob Canyons 73

Activities 81

4 **ZION GATEWAYS....89**

Welcome to Zion Gateways 90

Planning 93

Springdale 93

Hurricane............... 100

St. George.............. 101

Mount Carmel Junction 113

5 **BRYCE CANYON NATIONAL PARK ..115**

Welcome to Bryce Canyon National Park 116

Planning 119

Bryce Amphitheater 125

Under-the-Rim 141

Rainbow and Yovimpa Points...... 143

Bryce Canyon
City 144

Activities 148

6 **BRYCE CANYON
GATEWAYS** 155

Welcome to
Bryce Canyon
Gateways 156

Planning 159

Panguitch 160

Brian Head 163

Cedar City 166

Tropic 174

Escalante 175

INDEX 185

**ABOUT OUR
WRITER** 192

MAPS

Southwest Utah
Geologic Diagram ... 31

Zion Canyon 61

Kolob Canyons
Area 75

Kolob Terrace
Area 77

Springdale 95

St. George 103

Bryce
Amphitheater 126

Southern Bryce
Canyon 147

Cedar City 168

U.S. 89 and
Grand Staircase-
Escalante 177

EXPERIENCE ZION AND BRYCE CANYON NATIONAL PARKS

15 ULTIMATE EXPERIENCES

Zion and Bryce Canyon National Parks offer terrific experiences that should be on every traveler's list. Here are Fodor's top picks for a memorable trip.

1 Exploring Canyons

Hike through narrow slot canyons on trails or in water, rappel down from above, or climb canyon walls in the two national parks and nearby areas. (Ch. 3, 4, 5, 6)

2 Hiking Along a River

Strap on sturdy water shoes, and bring a walking stick and sense of adventure to hike up the Virgin River between the towering canyon walls of the Narrows. *(Ch. 3)*

3 Exploring on Horseback

Even beginners and kids can saddle up for a guided horseback ride in either Zion or Bryce; a trek in the latter allows for an up-close look at the amphitheater. *(Ch. 3, 5)*

4 Wandering Amid Hanging Gardens

Zion's "hanging gardens" are a must-see—lush flowers and ferns hang down from the cliff rocks, their roots fed by water dripping down the walls. See them on the Riverside Walk and by the Emerald Pools. *(Ch. 3)*

5 Hitting the Trail

Miles and miles of hiking, biking, and equestrian trails run through the national parks, forests, and nature preserves of southern Utah. Bring sturdy shoes! *(Ch. 3, 4, 5, 6)*

6 Bird-Watching

With more than 200 bird species identified at each park, birders will want to bring their binoculars to see which ones they can spot. Park websites have printable bird lists. *(Ch. 3, 5)*

7 Visiting a Desert Reserve

Experience a natural desert habitat at Red Cliffs Desert Reserve, where wildlife is abundant and trails welcome hikers, cyclists, and horseback riders. *(Ch. 4)*

8 Gazing at the Night Sky

Both parks are outstanding for stargazing. Bryce has night-sky ranger programs and a summer astronomy festival. Photograph the Milky Way at Kodachrome Basin State Park. *(Ch. 3, 5, 6)*

9 Experiencing Hoodoo Heaven

Bryce Canyon's thin, tall rock spires called "hoodoos" range from human height to 10 stories tall. They're found in a few other places in the world, including nearby Red Canyon, but nowhere as abundant as here. *(Ch. 5, 6)*

10 Seeing Sand Pipes

At Kodachrome Basin State Park, you can see 67 "sand pipes"—stone spires found nowhere else on Earth. Be sure to bring your camera to this park named after the color film. *(Ch. 6)*

11 Biking Through the Parks

Skip the shuttle lines on an invigorating bike ride along the main drives in either Zion or Bryce Canyon (or both!). You can catch a shuttle back if you need to. *(Ch. 3, 5)*

12 Driving Highway 12 Scenic Byway

The journey really is the destination on this epic, 123-mile route, an "All-American Road" that starts near Bryce Canyon and travels northeast. *(Ch. 5, 6)*

13 Exploring Hole-in-the-Rock Road

Retrace a pioneer route on this 60-mile dirt road from Escalante. It ends where, in 1878, Mormons worked for months chipping a hole through a canyon to make a "shortcut." *(Ch. 6)*

14 Peering Down from on High

The steep hike up to Angel's Landing rewards with jaw-dropping views down into Zion Canyon. If you have acrophobia, try to at least peek down into Bryce Canyon, steps from your car. *(Ch. 3, 5)*

15 Adventuring in the Backcountry

Intrepid adventurers can explore unique geological features like Zion's Subway and escape from the crowds overnight at primitive campgrounds in both parks. *(Ch. 3, 5)*

WHAT'S WHERE

1 Zion National Park. Utah's most visited park, like Las Vegas just three hours south, has an "over-the-top" feel, but its thrills come from starry skies, canyons, and other natural wonders.

2 Zion Gateways. There's just one in-park lodge, but amenities in nearby Springdale include a park shuttle. Tiny Hurricane is 22 miles west; 18 miles farther along is larger St. George. Mount Carmel Junction is 24 miles east of Zion en route to Bryce Canyon.

3 Bryce Canyon National Park. The smaller of the two parks can be experienced in a day, but longer stays allow for far more than just exploring hoodoos. It's 84 miles from Zion via Utah highways 9, 89, and 12.

4 Bryce Canyon Gateways. Panguitch, 24 miles northwest of Bryce Canyon, is also close to Cedar Breaks. West of Bryce are Brian Head (58 miles), a ski resort, and Cedar City (78 miles), a college town. Tiny Tropic is 10 miles east. Escalante, a recreation hub, is 48 miles north via Scenic Byway 12.

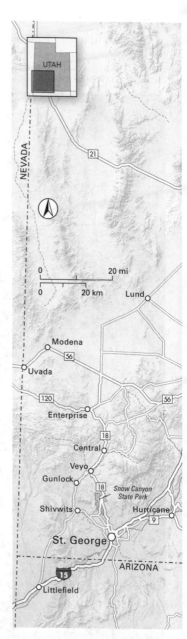

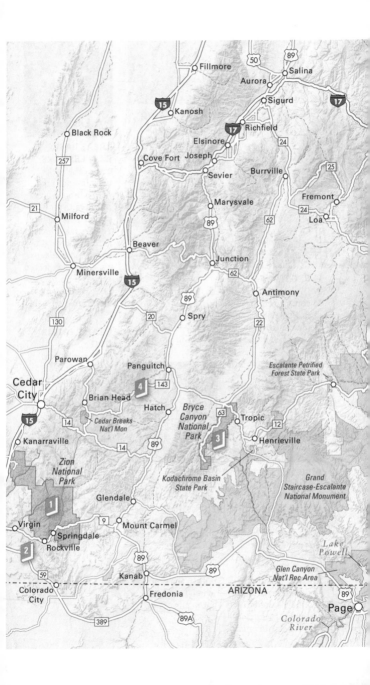

Birds, Reptiles, and Mammals of Zion and Bryce Canyon

GREAT BASIN RATTLESNAKE

One of the parks' most famous and feared inhabitants waits for its prey to approach. These snakes have excellent eyesight, so stay on trails to avoid an unexpected encounter, and seek immediate medical attention if bitten.

PEREGRINE FALCON

With wingspans of more than 3 feet, these falcons are often spotted near their nesting sites along cliffs and rocky ledges. Look for them in quieter, southern portions of Bryce Canyon and in the Fairyland Point area.

UTAH PRAIRIE DOG

They might look cuddly, but keep your distance. Some people make the mistake of feeding them, but doing so contributes to the rodent's lack of fear of humans. They carry diseases that could be lethal if they bite you.

BIGHORN SHEEP

Look for the rams (male) and ewes (female) in the Checkerboard Mesa area of Zion. The hollow-horned animals are especially active in fall. With padded hooves, they are uniquely suited to the steep, rocky slopes and canyons.

CLARK'S NUTCRACKER

Found throughout Bryce Canyon, these gray-and-black birds feed on the nuts from pine trees and also store tens of thousands of nuts in the ground, which facilitates the sprouting of new trees.

Gray fox

WATER OUZEL

Commonly known as the American dipper, this aquatic songbird is seen and heard by Zion's rivers. It stands alongside shallow waters, constantly dipping its head in to find food.

WILD TURKEY

On a Zion bus tour at dusk, a guide may point out turkey flocks, which appear as silhouettes in the trees above. Look for their colorful heads and dark bodies, which may have white tips on rich plumage.

WHIPTAIL LIZARD

Named for the way their tails swish side to side while running, these lizards are common to Zion. You'll spot them in desert scrub, grasslands, and pine forests.

GRAY FOX

Not uncommon but hard to spot, these foxes are mainly nocturnal. They have unique hooked claws and a rotating forearm that allows them to climb trees. They eat small mammals, insects, fruit, and nuts.

PRONGHORN ANTELOPE

With a spring that appears almost effortless as they bound across meadows of the high plateau of Bryce Canyon, the pronghorns are beautiful sights to behold.

Plants of Zion and Bryce Canyon

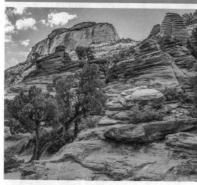

UTAH JUNIPER

Seen below the rim at Bryce Canyon and in the pygmy woodland of Zion, these short trees have edible blue berries that are used for medicinal purposes, for making beads, and for giving gin its unique flavor.

BIG SAGEBRUSH

This shrub grows in thick patches along trails in Zion. Rub the silvery, blue-green leaves to experience a fragrance described by one writer as "camphor blended with a touch of Christmas." Native Americans burn it to use the smoke for purification.

BRISTLECONE PINE

Bryce Canyon (at Yovimpa Point) is home to a pine that is more than 1,600 years old. The species' highly resinous wood and needles that don't fall off for 40 years help extend its longevity (the trees are among the oldest living organisms on Earth).

BRYCE CANYON PAINTBRUSH

This rare species of the figwort family grows—no taller than 6 inches—only in the park (hence its name). The delicate fuchsia flower blooms in May through August.

FREMONT COTTONWOOD

The presence of these trees indicates a long-term water source. Look for them along the Virgin River in Zion National Park. Younger trees have smooth bark; older ones develop deeply furrowed, whitish, cracked bark.

MAIDENHAIR FERN

One of 20 fern species in Zion, the delicate-leaved, moisture-loving plants can be seen in the hanging gardens that grow along sides of cliffs and near the Emerald Pools. Ferns reproduce via spores rather than seeds.

PINYON PINE

Found at Bryce Canyon, these slow-growing trees with crooked trunks have massive root systems. Their nutritious, valuable pine nuts drop in the fall. You're welcome to snack on them, but resist the temptation to harvest enough for a batch of pesto.

Fremont cottonwood

PONDEROSA PINE
You can easily identify these trees by their tall, straight trunks and reddish-orange, puzzle-piece-shaped bark that smells like vanilla. Named for their heavy "ponderous" wood, they're found throughout both national parks.

QUAKING ASPEN
Look for these trees on level, moist ground as well as on dry slopes. Their bark is smooth, and their leaves seem to quiver in the breeze—hence, their name.

ROCK COLUMBINE
The blue of these flowers contrasts with the red cliffs and soil of Bryce Canyon, making them one of the park's more distinctive plants. Highly regarded for their beauty, they've been used for ornamentation and perfumes for centuries.

Best Trails of Zion and Bryce Canyon

NAVAJO LOOP TRAIL

This steep route descends to Bryce's amphitheater via switchbacks and a narrow hallway of rock called Wall Street. Another trail back makes it an hour round-trip.

RIM TRAIL

A lovely stroll along the Bryce Amphitheater rim between Sunset and Sunrise points, this 1-mile trail is accessible to wheelchairs and strollers. Pets on leashes are welcome. Bring your camera in the evening for sunset photos of glowing hoodoos.

RIVERSIDE WALK

On this easy Zion stroll along the river, see wildflowers, hanging gardens, and the Narrows. Strollers can roll through without trouble; wheelchairs may need assistance. Round-trip, the 2.2-mile walk takes about 90 minutes.

QUEEN'S GARDEN TRAIL

The "essential Bryce sampler" trail descends 350 feet to the amphitheater, then to a tunnel and a ground-level view of the hoodoos. Although it gets crowded, it's a great route for families.

ANGELS LANDING TRAIL

One of Zion's most challenging hikes has switchbacks and a narrow path with chain handrails. It's not for kids or the height-averse, but as it's often crowded, many feel the 360-degree, top-side views are worth the trip.

PA'RUS TRAIL

Zion's only trail open to bikes and leashed pets is flat, paved, and easy. You'll catch views of the Watchman, the East and West temples, and Towers of the Virgin. Plus, you can dip your toes in the Virgin River.

THE NARROWS

Zion Canyon's narrowest section (20 to 30 feet) has 1,000-foot walls. Hikers wade through the Virgin River, following the trail up on a short or long trek; hiking from the top down requires rappelling and a permit.

PEEKABOO LOOP TRAIL

A steep, strenuous Bryce Canyon trail leads to the Wall of Windows and the Three Wise Men. Note that horses share the route and have the right-of-way. It takes at least four hours to hike the 5-mile trail.

EMERALD POOLS TRAIL

An easy, stroller- and wheelchair-friendly path starts across from Zion Lodge and passes waterfalls en route to the lower pool. It's all most impressive in spring when the snow melts; fall visits may be less vibrant.

CANYON OVERLOOK TRAIL

From the east entrance of Zion, this popular, 1-mile, round-trip trail takes about an hour. It's moderately steep, with a 180-foot elevation gain to reach the overlook and the breathtaking views. Come early for a parking spot; there's no shuttle service.

Welcome to Zion and Bryce Canyon

Look up, look down, repeat—as many times as necessary. Bryce Canyon and Zion are truly "vertical" experiences, with chasms and towers galore. Standing at the base of 2,000 feet of sheer rock in Zion's Virgin River Canyon, feel the cool canyon breezes. Even on summer's hottest days, cottonwoods rustle, and dozens of birds and mammals congregate in this "place of sanctuary" from the searing desert heat.

GEOLOGICAL HISTORY

Zion and Bryce offer an up-close look at millions of years of geological history. You'll be hard-pressed to find hoodoos like Bryce's anywhere on the planet. Two key steps in the Giant Staircase, these brilliant places are just a small section of a massive Southwest puzzle, where geologists are still unlocking the secrets to earth's history from the predinosaur eras to the present.

The Grand Staircase spans more than 150 miles, from the Paunsaugunt Plateau of Bryce Canyon (Yovimpa Point is 9,100 feet above sea level) to the Grand Canyon's south rim (6,800 feet). Deep canyons slice through, creating some places that are only nominally above sea level.

Bryce sits on top as the youngest sibling. A series of amphitheaters, its oldest layers are a mere 65 million years old. Erosion and frost-wedging (frequent freezing and thawing of moisture in rocks) has shaped the multihued rock into the canyons, arches, and spires of today.

Zion Canyon is one of the middle siblings; its oldest layers date back 240 million years. Zion was once a flat basin near sea level, but erosion from nearby mountains resulted in both its deep, slender gorges and its wide canyons.

PEOPLE OF THE LANDS

Evidence of human settlements in the lush, cool delta of Zion's Virgin River dates from as early as 500 AD, when the Virgin Anasazi (Ancestral Puebloan) and Parowan Fremont created year-round agricultural communities. Here, bow-and-arrow use became widespread. Both civilizations disappear from archaeological records about 1300 AD, apparently victims of droughts and intermittent catastrophic flooding. The Southern Paiute appear to have filled the void for some of the ensuing 500 years, before Euro-American explorations began to crisscross the Southwest on the Old Spanish Trail.

Brigham Young's Church of Jesus Christ of Latter-day Saints arrived in Utah in 1847, and by 1863, Isaac Behunin had built the first log cabin in Zion Canyon. Behunin, full of religious fervor, is credited with naming Zion. Mormon settlers added many of the religion-suf-fused names, such as the Three Patriarchs, Great White Throne, Angel's Landing, and at least three temples (East, West, and Sinawava).

Mormon settlers arrived in Bryce Canyon in the 1850s and 1860s, but their livestock grazing threatened the food sources of the Paiute tribe that hunted and gathered in the area. Wars ensued, many lives on both sides were lost, and most settlers left. Beginning in the early 1870s, the settlers returned and reestablished small farming communities, grazing their sheep and cows in the present-day park lands.

ESTABLISHING THE PARKS

In 1909, the area of pres-ent-day Zion was formally pre-served as the Mukuntuweap National Monument. After the government granted national park status to Zion in 1919, visitation grew through aggres-sive promotion, politicking, and development by the Union Pacific Railroad that slowly improved access to southern Utah—an important tourism destination on the railroad's western network. Construc-tion of the Zion–Mt. Carmel Highway in 1930 shortened travel times throughout the Southwest and increased the park's popularity.

Bryce Canyon first began to move into America's con-sciousness in the years after the Civil War. Grove Karl Gilbert wrote of "a perfect wilderness, the stunningest thing out of a picture." His words, along with sketches by John Weyss and increased Mormon settlement across southern Utah, attract-ed the interest of writers, artists, and traders.

When J. H. Humphrey became a National Park Service super-visor in 1915, extensive explo-rations of the area began—and rail barons took notice. Union Pacific officials saw Bryce as a key link for their growing Grand Canyon North Rim business, which had a longer tourism season than Yellowstone, their signature attraction at the time.

In 1927, Union Pacific and the NPS negotiated a historic swap. In exchange for more than 11 acres at Bryce Canyon, the park service agreed to build the Zion–Mt. Carmel tunnel. In 1928, Bryce Canyon was officially designated a national park. What resulted was the protection and preservation of what Bryce historian Nicholas Scrattish called "one of the world's best sites for an appreciation of the inexorable, titanic forces which have shaped the globe's surface."

A VAST REGION OF WONDERS

Zion and Bryce Canyon national parks are dual centerpieces of a massive wilderness stretching from Arizona's Grand Canyon to I–70, which crosses the center of Utah. The two parks are among the most recognized natural wonders in the Western United States as well as a microcosm of the region's geological and topographical diversity.

This is a land of adventure and contemplation, of adrenaline and retreat. It's not an either-or proposition: you can rejuvenate just as well while soaking at a luxury spa as you can by careening on a mountain bike down an alpine single-track. Ruins, petroglyphs, pioneer graffiti, and ghost towns— monuments to what once was—beckon new explorers.

The region's secrets reveal themselves to seekers, yet some mysteries remain elusive—the paradox of a bustling world hidden by the impression of silent, open space. Such contrasts have always attracted the curious. Famed explorer John Wesley Powell charted the uncharted; the young idealist and dreamer Everett Ruess left his wealthy family and lost himself without a trace in the canyons; the author and curmudgeon Ed Abbey found himself.

But that's the beauty of this place, the joy of choice in a land that confronts and challenges. We come, ostensibly, to escape; yet we really come to discover.

Zion and Bryce Canyon with Kids

National parks are great family destinations, and Zion and Bryce Canyon are no exceptions.

RANGER PROGRAMS

Before even arriving, kids can explore park websites as "virtual rangers." On arrival, stop by the visitor center to pick up the *Junior Ranger Handbook*. To learn about the park, kids ages 4 and up do activities from the guide and participate in ranger programs. Completing the required activities for their age group earns them the Junior Ranger badge. Since the program is offered at most national parks, kids can amass a collection of badges.

HIKING

Both Zion and Bryce have some great trails for kids; some are even stroller-friendly. Favorites at Zion are Pa'rus Trail, Lower Emerald Pools Trail, and Riverside Walk Trail. At Bryce, the Rim Trail is easiest but the Navajo/Queens Garden Loop is worth the effort to get down to the hoodoos—just plan for the uphill return. Note bathroom locations, and have kids stop before heading out on longer trails; it can be a long way back if nature calls during a hike. Bring plenty of water and snacks. (Having snacks on hand in general lets you avoid long snack-bar lines and keeps kids from getting "hangry.")

JUMP IN THE WATER

On a hot day, nothing beats a cool dip. At Zion, you can get wet in the river at the start of the Narrows or beneath a waterfall on Riverside Walk. (No swimming in the Emerald Pools, though.) Bryce Canyon doesn't have natural water features, but just outside the park, hotels all have seasonal outdoor pools. The venerable Ruby's Inn has an indoor pool, too.

ADVENTURES

Some kids get tired and bored after walking and hiking a while, even when they see things along the way with plenty of wow factor. If your kids want something more adventurous, check out horseback riding and canyoneering. Experienced guides from Canyon Trail Rides introduce kids as young as 7 to horseback riding at both parks. Start with the shortest tour if it's their first time. For canyoneering, the Zion Gurus expert guide service takes private groups for half- or full-day Adventure Canyon Quests at canyons near the park. Beginners will learn to use ropes and rappel from heights of 20 to 60 feet, and kids as young as 5 can participate.

What to Watch and Read

BETWEEN A ROCK AND A HARD PLACE

In 2003, while exploring southeastern Utah's canyons, Aron Ralston became trapped in a narrow crevasse. For five days. he struggled to break free from the 800-pound boulder that had crushed his arm, reflecting on his life as he faced his mortality. He eventually amputated his arm, rappelled to the canyon floor, and hiked out. His story was dramatized on the big screen in *127 Hours,*, starring James Franco.

BUTCH CASSIDY AND THE SUNDANCE KID

Paul Newman and Robert Redford starred in this classic 1969 western about Utah's most infamous outlaws. Katharine Ross played Etta, Sundance's lover. Most of the scenes were shot in and around Zion National Park and the nearby ghost town of Grafton.

CANYON WILDERNESS OF THE SOUTHWEST

Photographer Jon Ortner visited more than 50 locations in the canyon lands of Utah and Arizona, including 10 national parks, to shoot the more than 200 spectacularly scenic photos in this book.

DESERT SOLITAIRE

Edward Abbey wrote many books—both fiction and nonfiction—about the desert Southwest and this, published in 1968, is considered one of his best. It recounts his experiences during three seasons as a national park ranger.

IN SEARCH OF THE OLD ONES: EXPLORING THE ANASAZI WORLD OF THE SOUTHWEST

In this book, climber and mountaineer David Roberts takes readers on an archaeological expedition as he explores and uncovers Ancestral Puebloan sites and shares insights about their culture.

RED: PASSION AND PATIENCE IN THE DESERT

Prolific writer and naturalist Terry Tempest Williams shares an intimate look at the desert canyon lands of southern Utah where she has lived all her life. Her personal stories are entwined with historical accounts, giving a rich sense of place to the red-rock lands.

STANDING ON THE WALLS OF TIME: ANCIENT ART OF UTAH'S CLIFFS AND CANYONS

Author Kevin Jones, an archaeologist, teamed up with rock art researcher and photographer Layne Miller to create this fascinating book that showcases an array of rock art throughout the region.

TRAVEL SMART

Updated by
Shelley Arenas

★ **STATE CAPITAL:**
Salt Lake City

👤 **STATE POPULATION:**
3.2 million

💬 **LANGUAGE:**
English

$ **CURRENCY:**
U.S. dollar

📟 **AREA CODE:**
435

⚠ **EMERGENCIES:**
911

🚗 **DRIVING:**
On the right

⚡ **ELECTRICITY:**
120–220 v/60 cycles;
plugs have two or
three rectangular
prongs

🕓 **TIME:**
Mountain Time,
2 hours behind
New York

🌐 **WEB RESOURCES:**
www.nps.gov/brca/
index.htm,
www.brycecanyon.com,
www.zionpark.com,
www.visitutah.com

✈ **AIRPORTS:**
Salt Lake City
International Airport
(SLC), St. George
Regional Airport (SGU),
McCarren International
Airport (LAS)

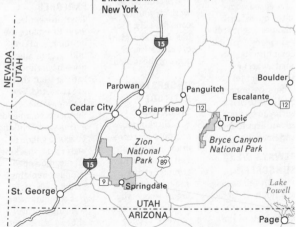

Know Before You Go

Several million people experience the wonders of Zion every year, and many venture on to see the hoodoos and heights of nearby Bryce Canyon. These tips will help you make the most of your visit while keeping the parks preserved for years to come.

COVID-19

In the early weeks of the COVID-19 pandemic, national parks, restaurants, and nearby services were closed fully or partially. When they reopened, there were new rules designed to limit the spread of the deadly virus. Although the rules may have eased, some of the operational changes might still be in place. Patience, flexibility, heightened awareness, and respect for others are important qualities to bring with you on your adventures to Zion and Bryce Canyon.

ALWAYS WEAR SUNSCREEN

The sun shines long and hot here. In fact, Utah is regularly named one of the top 10 sunniest states. Make sure you use sunscreen every day. Wearing a wide-brimmed hat and sunglasses with ultraviolet protection is essential, too. At high altitudes, UV exposure increases; most of the destinations in this book are situated at 3,000 to 10,000 feet. If you're tempted to work on your tan, consider this: Utah has the highest rate of skin cancer of any state in the nation.

UNDERSTAND ALTITUDE SICKNESS

Breathtaking views and outdoor recreation lose appeal fast when you have trouble getting enough oxygen to breathe normally; feel dizzy, nauseous, or weak; or get a headache. Altitude sickness begins to affect people at around 8,000 feet, so it's not uncommon to experience it at Bryce Canyon National Park. And, if you visit Cedar Breaks National Monument at 10,000 feet, the air will be even thinner. It's best to acclimate slowly, stay well hydrated, and descend as soon as you feel any symptoms rather than pushing on. Take at least a day to adjust to the thin mountain air before descending down the Bryce Canyon Amphitheater, since the only way out is back up, and altitude sickness could hit you then.

BE A SMART EXPLORER

There are endless ways to explore the outdoors—hiking, biking, climbing, horseback riding, rafting—but there are risks, too. The National Park Service recommends eating well, drinking at least a gallon of water a day, packing all recommended supplies, avoiding strenuous activities at midday, and wearing sturdy shoes. It's best not to head out alone, but if you do, let someone know where you're going and when you'll be back. If you get lost, just wait where you are for rescue. Make sure you have all necessary permits for backcountry and overnight trips, too.

MIND THE ELEMENTS

Hazardous conditions (fallen trees, rock slides, flash floods) can temporarily close roads, trails, and other areas of the parks at any time—though rangers try their best to keep delays short. All vistor centers have the most recent information about closures, as well as weather forecasts, which are important to check before heading out for a long hike or remote drive. Be prepared for sudden weather changes, and stay low if there's lightning. In winter, make sure your vehicle is prepared for cold-weather driving conditions, including sudden and heavy snowfall.

KEEP YOUR DISTANCE

Although you're unlikely to encounter dangerous animals, even if a creature seems tame or cute and cuddly, rely on your camera or binoculars to get a closer view. Never feed an animal, and if you see one that's sick or injured, contact a park ranger.

LEAVE NO TRACE

Within the national parks, it's illegal to pick wildflowers, take specimens, or otherwise disturb plants, rocks, or trees. Adopt a "leave-no-trace" policy: when you leave an area, take anything you brought with you and nothing more. Likewise, follow signs for closures and other regulations. These are in place for your safety; for the preservation of the wild and beautiful terrain; and, in some cases, to slow the effects of climate change, which is affecting the parks at an alarming rate.

KNOW THE LAWS

Utah has strict liquor laws, a result of the longstanding influence of the Mormon church, which forbids members from drinking alcohol. The maximum ABV limit for beer sold at grocery stores and beer bars is 5%; for anything stronger, you must go to a liquor store or a restaurant. Note, too, that most area bars don't stay open very late, and it's a bad idea to drink and drive: Utah has the nation's lowest allowable blood-alcohol level (.05%). In addition, marijuana is illegal except with a medical card.

PLAN AHEAD (BUT GO WITH THE FLOW)

For peak-season visits, reserve hotels or campsites well in advance, especially for in-park stays. Permits for exploring Zion's highly popular wilderness generally require a reservation weeks or months before arrival. That said, be open to spontaneous experiences. Although planning ahead can save time and prevent disappointment, leave room in your itinerary to follow a ranger recommendation or allow the pioneer spirit to take you on an improvised adventure.

Getting Here and Around

Separated by about 90 miles (along two-lane Scenic Highway 89), Zion and Bryce Canyon national parks attract millions of visitors annually despite their remote locations. Plan on at least three to five hours of driving from the closest major airports (Las Vegas and Salt Lake City), but savor the time spent on some of the Southwest's most memorable scenic drives.

Weather and elevation are two important considerations here. In summer, flash floods and incendiary heat (well over 110°F at low elevations) can be real perils. In winter, many back roads at the higher elevations are impassable due to snow and/or extreme cold.

Travel by horseback, bicycle, ATV, 4x4, and other means can be thrilling adventures, but be aware that natural elements can be deadly for the unprepared traveler. Gas stations in this part of the country may be more than 100 miles apart—and many places in this heavily Mormon part of the state are closed on Sunday.

 Air

Both Salt Lake City and Las Vegas airports are big international hubs served by all major airlines. Delta uses Salt Lake City as a western hub, but Las Vegas still has more options.

AIRPORTS

The major gateway to Utah is Salt Lake City International Airport, but a more convenient gateway to southern Utah, particularly if you're going only to Zion, is McCarran International Airport in Las Vegas. Bryce Canyon is equidistant between the two airports. Booming St. George's small airport is served by daily flights on several airlines from Salt Lake City, Phoenix, and Denver.

 Bus

From Las Vegas, you can take a Greyhound bus to St. George and then take a shuttle from there to Zion's main entrance. It makes for a long travel day, but overnighting in St. George is a good option. Tour buses and shuttles, including National Park Express, also run from Las Vegas to Zion and Bryce Canyon.

Between February and Thanksgiving (and during Christmas holidays), Zion Canyon Scenic Drive is closed to private vehicles (except for guests at Zion Lodge), and you must take the park shuttle. A second shuttle runs between Springdale and the park's south entrance. During the COVID-19 pandemic,

Southwest Utah
Geologic Diagram

ZION CANYON

GRAND CANYON

Paunsaugunt Plateau

BRYCE CANYON

PINK CLIFFS

GRAY CLIFFS

GRAND STAIRCASE

WHITE CLIFFS

CHOCOLATE CLIFFS

VERMILION CLIFFS

Kaibab Plateau

Paria Plateau

Marble Canyon

Getting Here and Around

a $1 reservation fee to ride the park shuttle was added to manage the number of riders and limit long waiting lines.

Adventure companies, such as Zion Guru and Zion Rock and Mountain Guides, also offer scheduled and on-demand shuttle rides to trailheads in Zion. At Bryce Canyon, a free park shuttle stops at many of the viewpoints and trailheads along the 18-mile main road, which is also open to private vehicles.

Car

Although park shuttles are handy, with all the spectacular scenery, you'll seldom get bored driving here. Note that the 120-mile drive from Las Vegas to St. George passes through extremely remote country, and the Virgin River Canyon near the Arizona/Utah border can make for treacherous driving, especially at night.

Before setting out, make sure your vehicle is in top condition. Pack flares or reflector triangles, jumper cables, an empty gas can, a fire extinguisher, a flashlight, a plastic tarp, blankets, water, and coins for phone calls (cell phones don't always work in high mountain areas).

CAR RENTALS

You can rent an economy car with air-conditioning, an automatic transmission, and unlimited mileage in Salt Lake City (a seven- to nine-hour drive from the parks) for about $35 a day and $175 a week, excluding taxes. Car rentals in Las Vegas can be less expensive than those in Salt Lake City, and the drive from Vegas to Zion is under three hours.

In Utah, you must be 21 and have a valid driver's license to rent a car; most companies also require a major credit card. If you're over 70, check the rental company's policy on overage drivers. You may pay extra for additional drivers and child car seats (though some companies don't charge for this), which are compulsory for children under 5; booster seats are required up to age 8. Non-U.S. residents need a reservation voucher, a passport, a driver's license, and a travel policy that covers each driver to pick up a car.

GASOLINE

In urban areas like St. George and Cedar City, gas prices are roughly similar to those elsewhere in the continental United States. Stations are plentiful, and most stay open late (some are open 24 hours). In rural and resort towns, as well as along remote stretches of I–15 or I–70, gas prices are considerably higher, stations are less frequent, and hours are more limited, particularly on Sunday. You can drive more than 100 miles on back roads without finding gas, so always keep your tank at least half full.

PARKING

All the hotels around Zion and Bryce Canyon provide free parking. Day visitors can park in visitor center parking lots.

ROAD CONDITIONS

Utah has some of the world's most spectacular vistas—and challenging driving. Routes range from multilane blacktop to narrow dirt roads; from twisting switchbacks bordered by guardrails to primitive tracks so narrow that you must back up to the edge of a steep cliff to make a turn. Scenic routes and lookout points are clearly marked, so you can readily take in the views.

Watch out for wildlife on the road. Exercise caution, not only to save an animal's life, but also to avoid damage to your car. In winter, expect snow and icy roads; it's best to have a four-wheel-drive vehicle or carry snow chains, especially in the Bryce Canyon area.

ROADSIDE EMERGENCIES

Call ☎ 911 for emergencies, such as an accident or a serious health concern. For automotive breakdowns, call a towing service or the Utah Highway Patrol.

RVS AND TRAILERS

Vehicles over 13'1" high, 40' long, and weighing more than 50,000 pounds are banned on the Zion–Mt. Carmel Highway, as are commerical trucks, vehicles towing a trailer with a combined length of 50 feet or more, and vehicles carrying hazardous materials. This eastern approach to Zion runs through a 90-year-old, mile-long tunnel that is too small for many contemporary RVs.

In addition, nearly every smaller RV, bus, dual-wheel truck, or trailer rig (essentially anything more than 7'10" wide or 11'4" high) will require an escort and must pay a $15 fee. Measurements include mirrors, awnings, rear-mounted tires, tow-hitches, etc. Each fee is good for two trips through the tunnel during a seven-day period, and the schedule for escorted vehicles is daily 8 am to 8 pm in summer (till 4:30 pm in winter).

 Train

Amtrak has service to Las Vegas, Salt Lake City, and St. George.

Essentials

📍 Accessibility

In Zion, both visitor centers, all shuttle buses, and Zion Lodge are fully accessible to people using wheelchairs. Several campsites are reserved for people with disabilities, and two trails—Pa'rus Trail and Riverside Walk—are generally accessible with some assistance.

Most Bryce Canyon facilities are accessible for travelers with disabilities, while others require some assistance. Because of the park's natural terrain, only a ½-mile section of the Rim Trail between Sunset and Sunrise points is wheelchair-accessible. The 1-mile Bristlecone Loop Trail at Rainbow Point has a hard surface and can be used with assistance, but several grades do not meet standards. Handicapped parking is marked at all overlooks and public facilities. Accessible campsites are available at Sunset Campground.

📍 Admission Fees

Entrance to Zion National Park is $35 per vehicle and includes the Kolob Canyons section, which has a separate entrance. People entering on foot or by bicycle pay $20 per person (youth 15 and under are free).

Motorcycles are $30. These fees are for a seven-day pass. An annual pass for Zion Canyon National Park, good for one year from the date of purchase, costs $70.

The fee for a seven-day pass at Bryce Canyon National Park is also $35 per vehicle, $30 for motorcycles, and $20 for pedestrians ages 16 and up (including visitors who ride the shuttle from the town) and bicyclists. An annual pass for Bryce Canyon National Park, good for one year from the date of purchase, costs $40.

🍴 Dining

Utah doesn't have a signature cuisine, per se; rather, its restaurants borrow from a number of sources. American dishes are most common, followed closely by those with Mexican or Southwestern influences. Because this is a conservative state, don't presume a restaurant serves beer, much less wine or cocktails, especially in smaller towns. Also, many places close on Sunday.

ZION RESTAURANTS

The gateway to Zion is the town of Springdale, which has more services and amenities—including a broad spectrum of resorts, boutique inns, and bed-and-breakfasts— than ever. What's more, although it's in the middle of the desert, with midsummer temperatures often in the 100-plus°F range, there's a truly impressive abundance of fresh fish, flavorful natural ingredients, and vegetarian options in Springdale's restaurants.

The Red Rock Grill is the only full-service restaurant in the only full-service accommodation (Zion Lodge) in Zion National Park. It offers the warm stone-and-timber comfort that makes the West's best park lodges such important stops. There's also a seasonal snack bar café at the lodge for more casual fare.

In Springdale, dawn breaks with the smell of fresh-roasted coffee and fresh-baked pastries at multiple coffee shops and restaurants. Oscar's Café (for huevos rancheros) and the Park House Cafe (for vegan and vegetarian meals) are among the interesting choices here. King's Landing Bistro gets rave reviews for delicious food, and the views are excellent, too. To the east, Mount Carmel Junction is the first community you reach off the park entrance road—it's a one-stop-sign sort of place, without the charm or choices of Springdale.

BRYCE CANYON RESTAURANTS

You come to Bryce for hoodoos, not haute cuisine. That being said, Bryce Canyon Lodge serves above-average cuisine and has an authentic park lodge atmosphere. Note that the convenience stores in the immediate vicinity of the park and grocery stores in Tropic, Bryce Canyon City (Ruby's Inn), and Panguitch are the only outposts for food and sundries. Plan accordingly.

The closest gateway towns, including Panguitch, only have a few cafes and most shut down in winter. There is no equivalent to Springdale near Bryce, but if you travel farther to Cedar City, you'll find some excellent eateries there. Also, throughout the region be on the lookout for locally grown produce and fresh-baked pies.

PAYING

Most restaurants take credit cards, but some smaller places may not. It's worth asking. Waiters expect a 20% tip at high-end restaurants; some add an automatic gratuity for groups of six or more.

RESERVATIONS AND DRESS

Almost every restaurant is family-friendly, and dress is hiker-casual. Prices are reasonable, though they inch higher

Essentials

in and near the national parks. Be advised that although Zion is increasingly a four-season community, many businesses still shut their doors through the coldest months (January and February). None of the restaurants near Zion and Bryce take reservations, and you might have to wait for a table during the busy summer and early fall seasons.

MEALS AND MEALTIMES
Zion's Red Rock Grill opens at 6:30 am for breakfast and serves dinner until 10 pm. The dining room is closed for periods during the rest of the day, but the lounge is open for a quick mid-afternoon bite. At Bryce Canyon, breakfast starts at 7:30 am, and dinner service ends at 8 pm. Restaurants in the smaller gateway towns often close early, too (though some in St. George and Cedar City serve till 10 pm), and not all are open on Sunday.

WINES, BEER, AND SPIRITS
Despite what you may have heard, it's not hard to get a drink in Utah, though you must be 21 to purchase or consume alcohol. Many restaurants have licenses that allow them to serve wine and beer—and occasionally liquor—with a meal. Others allow you to bring your own wine, but may charge a corkage fee. Call ahead, though, as lots of regulations cover brown bagging. Still other restaurants—generally those that cater to families—opt not to carry a liquor license, so check ahead if you're set on having a drink with your meal.

Beer with 5% alcohol by volume is available in grocery and some convenience stores. For anything else, you'll have to go to a state liquor store. The closest ones to the parks are in Cedar City and Panguitch. They are closed on Sunday, Election Day, and holidays. Note that Utah recently lowered its maximum legal blood-alcohol level in drivers from 0.08% to 0.05%, giving it the lowest and strictest DUI threshold in the country.

SMOKING
Smoking is banned in all restaurants and bars.

What It Costs			
$	$$	$$$	$$$$
AT DINNER			
under $16	$16– $22	$23– $30	over $30

➕ Health and Safety

For summer backcountry hikes, rangers warn about heat stroke, dehydration, disorientation, flash floods, cougars, bears, lightning, rattlesnakes, and a few other hazards. In winter, hypothermia and blizzards are the biggest dangers. But threats are just as real in the front-country. Every year, day visitors to both parks slip on rocks, trip on uneven surfaces, become dehydrated, suffer from too much sun, and have heart and/or breathing problems due to the extreme altitude. Use common sense, know your limitations, and don't be afraid to ask for help.

Bryce Canyon publishes a list of the top 10 causes for injuries in the park. These include unsafe driving, climbing or skiing off the canyon rim, feeding animals, ignoring extreme weather, dehydration, leaving the trail, over-exhaustion, and choosing the wrong footwear. Similar hazards have caused injuries at Zion, where flash floods and falls off cliffs have also led to fatalities.

A novel coronavirus brought all travel to a virtual standstill in 2020. Although the illness is mild in most people, some experience severe and even life-threatening complications.

Once travel started up again, albeit slowly and cautiously, travelers were asked to be careful about hygiene and to avoid any unnecessary travel, especially if they are sick.

Older adults, especially those over 65, have a greater chance of having severe complications from COVID-19. The same is true for people with weaker immune systems or those living with some types of medical conditions, including diabetes, asthma, heart disease, cancer, HIV/AIDS, kidney disease, and liver disease. Starting two weeks before a trip, anyone planning to travel should be on the lookout for some of the following symptoms: cough, fever, chills, trouble breathing, muscle pain, sore throat, new loss of smell or taste. If you experience any of these symptoms, you should not travel at all.

During travel, do your best to avoid contact with people showing symptoms. Wash your hands often with soap and water. Limit your time in public places, and, when you are out and about, wear a cloth face mask that covers your nose and mouth. Indeed, a mask may be required in some places, such as on airplanes and park shuttles and in restaurants (except when eating) and

Essentials

visitor centers. You may wish to bring extra supplies, such as disinfecting wipes, hand sanitizer (12-ounce bottles were allowed in carry-on luggage at this writing), and a first-aid kit with a thermometer.

Given how abruptly travel was curtailed in March 2020, it is wise to consider protecting yourself by purchasing a travel insurance policy that will reimburse you for any costs resulting from COVID-19–related cancellations. Not all travel insurance policies protect against pandemic-related cancellations, so always read the fine print.

 Immunizations

There are no immunization requirements for visitors traveling to the United States for tourism.

Lodging

IN ZION

Since Zion Lodge (the only in-park lodging option) has fewer than 80 rooms, getting a reservation inside the park can be harder than finding a beer at noon on a Sunday in southern Utah. Plan well ahead—by as much as six to nine months,

in fact—to ensure a stay in this landmark property near the Virgin River. Designed by Gilbert Stanley Underwood, the original main building was built in 1924–25 and burned down in 1966, but it was rebuilt within 100 days. The rebuilt version, however, was not consistent with the original's look, so the lodge was restored in 1990 to the original style. Some of the adjacent cabins, however, are originals from the late 1920s.

If you can't get a room in the park, try the gateway community of Springdale, which has everything from small motels to quaint bed-and-breakfasts to upscale hotels with modern amenities and riverside rooms. To save the most, consider staying in Hurricane, about 20 miles west of the park. Another 20 miles beyond Hurricane is St. George, a booming community with scores of options for every budget.

IN BRYCE CANYON

For many who explore the West's national parks, staying in a park lodge is the only way to go. Bryce Canyon Lodge may not have as much charm or history as other such lodges, but it's the best option here, hands down, in terms of price, location, food, and character.

The park's closest community, Bryce Canyon City, has Ruby's

Inn and two sister hotels. Ruby's is a monstrosity, with nearly 400 rooms and a theme-park feel that overwhelms its historical importance (for years, it was literally the only place to stay).

Southwestern Utah is steeped in pioneer heritage, and many older homes are also bed-and-breakfasts. There are also a number of motels in small towns and unincorporated areas within an hour of the park, including the ski resort community of Brian Head, the village of Panguitch, Escalante, and Cedar City.

Camping is a great option, though freezing nights are possible at any time of the year given the elevation (which ranges from 6,600 in the amphitheater to nearly 8,000 feet at the park's entrance). If you're stocking up for your campsite or kitchenette, hit the groceries in Panguitch or Cedar City for the best variety and prices.

FACILITIES

You can assume that all rooms have private baths, phones, TVs, and air-conditioning, unless otherwise indicated. Breakfast is noted when it is included in the rate, but it's not a typical perk at most Utah hotels. There are a few hotels with pools.

PARKING

Parking is typically free at the area's hotels.

PRICES

Rates at the in-park lodges are highest in summer. During winter, they drop 20%–40%. There are similar off-season discounts at many motels and hotels in the gateway communities, with the exception of the Brian Head area, where winter brings visitors who come to hit the slopes. Smaller lodgings in some gateway towns close for at least a couple months in winter.

RESERVATIONS

For both Zion and Bryce, reserve rooms and campsites ahead for the summer high season (in-park accommodations reservations need to be made months in advance). If you're willing to stay upward of an hour away from the parks, you may be able to get same-day reservations. The properties may have fewer amenities but also lower rates.

What It Costs			
$	$$	$$$	$$$$
FOR TWO PEOPLE			
under $125	$125–$175	$176–$225	over $225

Essentials

📷 Packing

While it's best not to over pack, especially when heading into the parks via shuttles and out onto trails, it's important to be prepared for the weather and for both planned and spontaneous activities.

Sun protection is essential, including sun block, sunglasses, and hats. In summer, pack at least one lightweight rain jacket and a pair of long pants, especially if you plan to do any horseback riding. Capris, shorts, and zip-off pants are good options for hot days. For the shoulder season, dressing in layers makes it easy to adapt to temperature changes. In winter, especially for Bryce Canyon visits, you'll need a warm waterproof jacket, knit hat, gloves, and long underwear. Sturdy footwear is necessary for nearly all activities. Also bring a pair of closed-toed water shoes (these can be rented from outfitters) for hiking up the Narrows or river rafting.

A daypack is also a must (practice with it before traveling to make sure it's comfortable to carry). In addition to sunscreen and extra clothing layers, carry snacks and plenty of water: a gallon per person per day is recommended; you can fill up as needed when in developed areas, but don't head out to the backcountry with an empty bottle. On trips long or short, it's also good to have water-purification tablets, bug spray, a small first-aid kit, flashlight, a camera, and lightweight binoculars. For longer treks, bring meals as well as snacks, a tablecloth, a head lamp and star chart if you plan to be out in the evening, and plastic bags to bring back garbage and used toilet paper (please don't leave it in the park!). Other handy things include a park guide and other special-interest books and small resealable plastic bags for protecting tech items in a sudden downpour or when trekking through rivers.

🌐 Passport

All visitors to the United States require a passport that is valid for six months beyond your expected period of stay.

📍 Permits

In Zion, permits are required for backcountry camping and overnight climbs. The maximum size of a group hiking into the backcountry is 12 people. The cost for a permit for 1 to 2 people is $15; for 3 to 7 people, $20; and for 8 to 12 people, $25. Permits are limited, and demand is high; online reservations are your best chance to get one. Permits and hiking information are available at the Zion Canyon Visitor Center.

In Bryce, a $5 backcountry permit, available from the visitor center, is required for camping in the park's interior, allowed only on Under-the-Rim Trail and Riggs Spring Loop, both south of Bryce Point. Campfires are not permitted.

$ Taxes

Sales tax is 4.85% in Utah. Most areas have additional local sales and lodging taxes, which can be quite significant. For example, in Salt Lake City, the combined sales tax is 7.75%. Sales tax is reduced for some items, such as groceries.

$ Tipping

At least 15% is customary in restaurants, but 18% to 20% is increasingly the norm. For coat checks and bellhops, $1 per coat or bag is the minimum. Taxi drivers expect 10% to 15%, depending on where you are. In resort towns, ski technicians, sandwich makers, coffee baristas, and the like also appreciate tips.

Visa

Except for citizens of Canada and Bermuda, most visitors to the United States must have a visa. If you are from one of the 38 designated members of the Visa Waiver Program, then you only require an ESTA (Electronic System for Travel Authorization) as long as you are staying for 90 days or less. However, some changes were made in the Visa Waiver Program in 2015, and nationals of Visa-Waiver nations who have traveled to Iran, Iraq, Libya, Somalia, Sudan, Syria, or Yemen no longer qualify for ESTA. Also, if you have been denied a visa to visit the United States, your application for the ESTA program most likely will be denied.

When to Go

Low Season: November through February is the low season at Zion, though the park gets a lot of visitors during the week from Christmas to New Year's, and it runs the park shuttle then. In smaller gateway towns, some accommodations and eateries shut down during

Essentials

Tipping Guides for Zion and Bryce Canyon

Bartender	$1–$5 per round of drinks, depending on the number of drinks
Bellhop	$1–$5 per bag, depending on the level of the hotel
Coat Check	$1–$2 per coat
Hotel Concierge	$5 or more, depending on the service
Hotel Doorstaff	$1–$5 for help with bags or hailing a cab
Hotel Maid	$2–$5 a day (in cash, preferably daily since cleaning staff may be different each day you stay)
Hotel Room Service Waiter	$1–$2 per delivery, even if a service charge has been added
Porter at Airport or Train Station	$1 per bag
Restroom Attendants	$1 or small change
Skycap at Airport	$1–$3 per bag checked
Spa Personnel	15%–20% of the cost of your service
Taxi Driver	15%–20%
Tour Guide	10%–15% of the cost of the tour, per person
Valet Parking Attendant	$2–$5, each time your car is brought to you
Waiter	15%–20%, with 20% being the norm at high-end restaurants; nothing additional if a service charge is added to the bill

this time. Low season at Bryce Canyon runs through March.

Shoulder Season: Both parks are less crowded in the spring and early fall. Note, though, that higher-elevation Bryce Canyon does get snow in early spring, so trails might still be covered.

High Season: From Memorial Day to Labor Day, the parks are busiest and offer the most activities. The gateway town of Brian Head, however, is busiest in winter thanks to its ski resort.

WEATHER

Summer in Zion is hot and dry except for sudden cloudbursts, which can cause flash floods (but can also create spectacular waterfalls!). Expect afternoon thunderstorms between July and September. Even in the height of summer, there is ample shade on the canyon floor. Winters are mild at lower desert elevations, so consider planning a shoulder-season visit. Expect winter-driving conditions and very few park programs from November through March. Nevertheless, winter is a wonderful, solitary time to see the canyons.

Around Bryce Canyon National Park and the nearby Cedar Breaks National Monument area, elevations approach and surpass 9,000 feet, making for temperamental weather, intermittent and seasonal road closures, and downright cold nights well into June. At this altitude, the warm summer sun is perfectly balanced by the coolness of the alpine forests during the day. Bryce gets much more snow than Zion, so keep that in mind when you plan a winter trip.

On the Calendar

January

Panguitch Lake Ice Fishing Derby. The first Saturday in January, anglers fish for rainbow trout under thick ice and then take the fish they reel in to be weighed and measured for prizes. The hockey slapshot contest is another fun activity on the ice. ⊕ *panguitch.com/panguitch-lake-big-fish-derby*

February

Bryce Canyon Winter Festival. Ruby's Inn hosts this three-day festival, held over Presidents' Day weekend, for snow lovers, featuring ski races, Nordic skiing tours, snowshoeing, archery, and stargazing. Inside, enjoy arts and crafts, photography workshops, yoga, dancing, and more. ⊕ *www.rubysinn.com/bryce-canyon-winter-festival*

April

St. George StreetFest. On the first Friday evening of the month, from April through October, downtown St. George is the place to be, with free live music, an outdoor market, food trucks, a beer garden, and a silent dance party. ⊕ *stgeorge-streetfest.com*

St. George Art Festival. Held the Friday and Saturday before Easter in St. George's Town Square, this popular festival has an artisan market, kids activities, food booths, and plenty of entertainment—from music to cowboy poetry. ⊕ *www.sgartfestival.com*

May

Festival of the Americas. At the Kayenta Art Village, near ancestral lands of the Paiute, celebrate traditions of Native Americans, Latinos, and other early cultures in late May. There's music, theater, ethnic foods, artisans, and pow-wow activities like drumming circles and friendship dances. ⊕ *www.kayentaarts.com/festival-of-the-americas*

Memorial Day—August

Bryce Canyon Country Rodeo. Watch, or even ride, in the rodeo every Wednesday to Saturday throughout most of the summer at the Ruby's Inn rodeo grounds. ⊕ *www.rubysinn.com/activities-in-bryce-canyon/utah-rodeo*

June

Bryce Canyon Astronomy Fest.
Activities at this four-day, late-June event include ranger talks, guided walks, and model-rocket building. In the evening, learn more about the night sky through telescopes. ⊕ www.nps.gov/brca/planyour-visit/astrofest.htm

Panguitch Valley Balloon Rally.
Hot-air balloons fill the skies with color in this two-day, late-month event. At night, Main Street features a "balloon glow." ⊕ panguitch.com/panguitch-valley-balloon-rally

Quilt Walk Festival. One hard winter, early pioneers discovered they could travel to get food and supplies by laying down quilts to walk over heavy snow. A quilt show, pioneer home tours, and more commemorate that historical event in Panguitch over four days the second week in June. ⊕ www.quiltwalk.org

June–October

Utah Shakespeare Festival. It's been a Shakespeare extravaganza in Cedar City since 1962, with shows running from summer to fall at three venues, including an open-air replica of the bard's Globe Theatre. ⊕ www.bard.org

July

Bryce Canyon Geology Festival (GeoFest). Geologist-guided tours, exhibits, and plein art painting are some of the activities at this fun, informative, two-day festival held in late July. ⊕ www.nps.gov/brca/annual-geology-festival.htm

Utah Midsummer Renaissance Faire. Travel back to medieval times, with lively entertainment, unique wares, and hearty feasting fare at a four-day, mid-July event. ⊕ www.umrf.net

September

Dixie Roundup Rodeo. Put on your favorite cowboy or cowgirl attire and head to St. George's Sun Bowl for all the best in rodeo fun, from bull riding to mutton busting. The four-day event takes place the second week of the month. ⊕ www.stgeorgelions.com/wp/?page_id=178

Escalante Canyons Art Festival. Near the Grand Staircase–Escalante Monument, this art and literary gathering—held over two weeks, starting mid-month—highlights the area's history, paying tribute to the legendary young poet-artist Everett Ruess, who disappeared near here in 1934. ⊕ escalantecanyonsartfestival.org

On the Calendar

Kayenta Acoustic Roots Music for ALL Festival. At this four-day, mid-month event, nicknamed the KARMA Fest, the combination of stunning outdoor setting and diverse acoustic music naturally brings on the good vibes. ⊕ *www.kayentaarts. com/karma-fest/*

Zion Canyon Music Festival. The long-running, weekend festival is held late in the month at a Springdale amphitheater just minutes from the park entrance. Bands play folk, blues, rock, and more. ⊕ *zion-canyonmusicfestival.com*

October

Cedar City Livestock & Heritage Festival. Celebrating all things agricultural, this two-day, late-month festival includes a sheep parade down Cedar City's main drag, a tractor-pull, a draft-horse show, a Dutch oven–cooking contest, cowboy poetry, and music. ⊕ *www. cedarlivestockfest.com*

Scarecrow Walk and Haunted Canyon. See scarecrows and walk through a canyon decorated with skeletons and other spooky things at St. George's Red Hills Desert Garden during the last half of October. ⊕ *re-dhillsdesertgarden.com*

November

Holiday Lights at Red Hills Desert Garden. Beginning the night after Thanksgiving and running through New Year's Eve, the garden is filled with twinkling lights to celebrate the season. ⊕ *www.wcwcd.org/event/light-ing-up-red-hills-desert-garden*

December

Christmas Bird Count. Learn about the birds of Bryce Canyon, and become a citizen scientist by helping count them in the park the Saturday before Christmas. Coordinated by the Audubon Society, this event has been held nationwide since 1900. ⊕ *www.nps.gov/ brca/learn/nature/brcacbc.htm*

Contacts

 Air

AIRPORTS McCarran International Airport (LAS). ✉ 5757 Wayne Newton Blvd., Las Vegas ☎ 702/261–5211 ⊕ www.mccarran.com. **Salt Lake City International Airport (SLC).** ✉ 3920 W. Terminal Dr., Salt Lake City ☎ 801/575–2400 ⊕ www.slcairport.com. **St. George Regional Airport (SGU).** ✉ 4550 S. Airport Pkwy., St. George ☎ 435/627–4080 ⊕ www.flysgu.com.

AIRLINES Alaska Airlines. ☎ 800/252–7522 ⊕ www.alaskaair.com. **American Airlines.** ☎ 800/433–7300 ⊕ www.aa.com. **Delta Airlines.** ☎ 800/221–1212 for U.S. reservations, 800/241–4141 for international reservations ⊕ www.delta.com. **Frontier.** ☎ 801/401–9000 ⊕ www.flyfrontier.com. **jetBlue.** ☎ 800/538–2583 ⊕ www.jetblue.com. **Southwest Airlines.** ☎ 800/435–9792 ⊕ www.southwest.com. **United Airlines.** ☎ 800/864–8331 U.S. and Canada reservations ⊕ www.united.com.

 Bus

Greyhound. ☎ 800/231–2222 ⊕ www.greyhound.com. **National Park Express.** ☎ 702/948–4190 ⊕ www.nationalparkexpress.com. **St. George Shuttle.** ✉ 1275 E Red Hills Pkwy., St. George ☎ 800/933–8320, 435/628–8320 ⊕ www.stgshuttle.com. **Zion Guru Shuttle.** ✉ 792 Zion Park Blvd., Springdale ☎ 432/632–0432 ⊕ www.zionguru.com/hiking-shuttles. **Zion Rock and Mountain Guides Shuttle.** ✉ 1458 Zion Park Blvd., Springdale ☎ 435/772–3303 ⊕ www.zionrockguides.com.

 Car

ROAD CONDITIONS Nevada Department of Transportation. ☎ 511 ⊕ www.nvroads.com. **Utah Department of Transportation.** ☎ 511 ⊕ www.commuterlink.utah.gov.

MAJOR CAR RENTAL AGENCIES Advantage. ☎ 800/777–5500 ⊕ www.advantage.com. **Alamo.** ☎ 844/354–6962 ⊕ www.alamo.com. **Avis.** ☎ 800/633–3469 ⊕ www.avis.com. **Budget.** ☎ 800/218–7992 ⊕ www.budget.com. **Hertz.** ☎ 800/654–3131 ⊕ www.hertz.com. **National Car Rental.** ☎ 844/382–6875 ⊕ www.nationalcar.com.

Train

Amtrak. ☎ 800/872–7245 ⊕ www.amtrak.com.

Did You Know?

With multiple and surprisingly diverse ecosystems, Zion National Park contains roughly 85% of the flora and fauna that can be found throughout the state of Utah.

ZION NATIONAL PARK

Updated by
Shelley Arenas

⛺ Camping	🛏 Hotels	🎯 Activities	👁 Scenery	👥 Crowds
★★★★★	★★★★☆	★★★★★	★★★★★	★☆☆☆☆

WELCOME TO ZION NATIONAL PARK

TOP REASONS TO GO

★ **Eye candy:** Just about every trail culminates in an astounding view of pink, orange, and crimson rock formations.

★ **Peace and quiet:** From February through November, cars aren't allowed on Zion Canyon Scenic Drive, so this section of the park stays relatively peaceful.

★ **Botanical wonderland:** Zion Canyon has over 1,000 species of plants, more than anywhere else in Utah.

★ **Animal tracks:** Zion's expansive hinterlands are full of furry, scaly, or feathered residents such as deer, elk, lizards, and birds of prey.

★ **Unforgettable canyoneering:** Rugged slot canyons are perfect for scrambling, rappelling, climbing, and descending.

1 Zion Canyon. For most people, Zion is defined by this area, where the backcountry is accessible via the West Rim Trail and the Narrows and 2,000-foot cliffs rise all around.

2 Kolob Canyons. Zion's northwestern corner is a secluded 30,000-acre wonderland accessible only via a special entrance. Don't miss the West Temple and Kolob Arch.

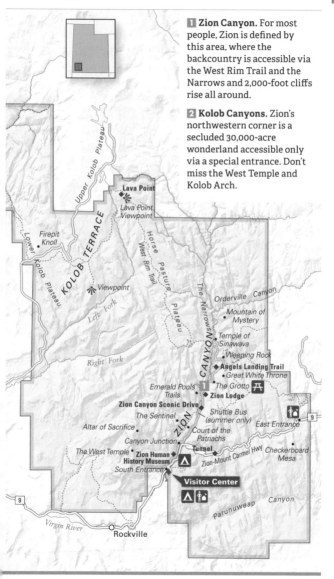

The walls of Zion Canyon soar more than 2,000 feet above the valley, but it's the character, not the size, of the sandstone forms that defines the park's splendor. The domes, fins, and blocky massifs bear the names and likenesses of cathedrals and temples, prophets and angels.

But for all Zion's grandeur, trails that lead deep into side canyons and up narrow ledges on the sheer canyon walls reveal a subtler beauty. Tucked among the monoliths are delicate hanging gardens, serene spring-fed pools, and shaded spots of solitude. So diverse is this place that 85% of Utah's flora and fauna species are found here. Some, like the tiny Zion snail, appear nowhere else in the world.

At the genesis of Zion is the Virgin River, a tributary of the mighty Colorado. It's hard to believe that this muddy little stream is responsible for carving the great canyon you see, until you witness it transformed into a rumbling red torrent during spring runoff and summer thunderstorms. Cascades pour from the cliff tops, clouds float through the canyon, and then the sun comes out, and you know you're walking in one of the West's most loved and sacred places. If you're lucky, you may catch such a spectacle, but when the noisy waters run thick with debris, make sure that you keep a safe distance—these "flash floods" can, and do, kill.

The park comprises two distinct sections—Zion Canyon, and the Kolob Plateau and Canyons. Most people restrict their visit to the better-known Zion Canyon, especially if they have only one day to explore, but the Kolob area has much to offer and should not be missed if time allows. There's little evidence of Kolob's beauty from the entrance point off Interstate 15, but once you negotiate the first switchback on the park road, you are hit with a vision of red rock cliffs shooting out of the earth. As you climb in elevation, you are treated first to a journey through these canyons, then with a view into the chasm. Due to geography—no roads connect Zion Canyon with Kolob Canyon—and to access points that are far apart, it is difficult to explore both sections in one day.

Great Itineraries

ZION IN ONE DAY

Begin at the **Zion Canyon Visitor Center**, where outdoor exhibits showcase park geology, wildlife, history, and trails. Get a taste of what's in store by viewing the distant Towers of the Virgin, then head to the **Court of the Patriarchs** viewpoint to take photos and walk the short path. Take the shuttle (or drive in December or January) to **Zion Lodge**, and hike a trail to the stunning **Emerald Pools**. The popular Lower Pool Trail branches off into Middle Pool and Upper Pool trails for those with more time. Ride the next shuttle to the end of the road, where the paved, accessible **Riverside Walk** delivers you to the gateway of the canyon's Narrows.

Reboard the shuttle to return to the visitor center to pick up your car (or continue driving). Travel the beautiful **Zion–Mount Carmel Highway**, with its long, curving tunnel. At the park's east entrance, turn around; on your return trip, stop for the short hike up to **Canyon Overlook**. In the evening, attend a ranger program.

ZION IN THREE DAYS

Take at least one signature hike, but slow down, and don't attempt the Zion–Mount Carmel Highway or push yourself to do the Riverside Walk on Day 1. Do, however, stop at the **visitor center** to determine your plans for Day 2, especially if you are interested in an expedition that requires a permit.

Start Day 2 with a daybreak drive along the **Zion–Mt. Carmel Highway**. As the sun rises behind you, hike the short **Canyon Overlook Trail** for stunning pictures of Zion Canyon's south end. Return through the tunnel, leave your car at **Canyon Junction**, and take the shuttle all the way to the **Temple of Sinawava** (en route, pick up a picnic lunch or snacks at Zion Lodge). The **Riverside Walk** is a peaceful, milelong, waterside wander that deposits you at the mouth of the **Narrows**. This is Zion's most famous attraction. You don't need a permit or special training to wade in and wander upriver, just heavy boots or neoprene shoes and maybe a walking stick. Whether you follow the river around one bend or for 5 miles, you'll be dwarfed (and humbled) by the surrounding 2,000-foot cliffs.

On Day 3, head north to **Kolob Canyon**, where the **Taylor Creek Trail** follows the riverbed past two homesteaders' cabins to the memorable **Double Arch Alcove**. This relatively flat hike also showcases an ever-narrowing "finger" canyon. From here, explore **Cedar City**; if it's summer, end the day with a Shakespearean play at the outdoor theater on the Southern Utah University campus.

AVERAGE HIGH/LOW TEMPERATURES (FAHRENHEIT)					
JAN.	FEB.	MAR.	APR.	MAY	JUNE
52/29	57/31	63/36	73/43	83/52	93/60
JULY	AUG.	SEPT.	OCT.	NOV.	DEC.
100/68	97/66	91/60	78/49	63/37	53/30

Planning

When to Go

Zion is the most heavily visited national park in Utah, receiving 4.5 million visitors each year. Locals used to call the spring and fall the shoulder seasons because traffic would drop off from the highly visited summer months. Not so much anymore. These days the park is busy from March through November.

Summer in the park is hot and dry, punctuated by sudden cloudbursts that can create flash flooding and spectacular waterfalls. Expect afternoon thunderstorms between July and September. Whether the day starts out sunny or not, wear sunscreen and drink lots of water, even if you aren't exerting yourself or spending much time outside. The sun is very powerful at this elevation.

Winters are mild at lower desert elevations. You can expect to encounter winter driving conditions from November to mid-March, and although many park programs are suspended in winter, it is a wonderful and solitary time to see the canyons.

■TIP→ **The temperature in Zion often exceeds 100°F in July and August.**

Getting Here and Around

AIR
The nearest commercial airport, with direct flights from a number of western U.S. hubs, is an hour away in St. George, Utah. It's about a 3-hour drive to the nearest major airport, McCarran in Las Vegas, Nevada, and a 4½-hour drive to Salt Lake City's airport.

BUS
Greyhound buses run to the gateway towns of St. George and Cedar City. From either, you can catch a shuttle to the park. In addition, tour buses run to the park from Las Vegas, about 3 hours away. You don't need a vehicle to explore the main area of the

park. Indeed, most of the year, you're not allowed to bring one in, except when staying at Zion Lodge. Instead, the park is served by two shuttle lines. In the town of Springdale, a free shuttle runs to the park entrance. You can leave your car at your lodging and reach the park in minutes from the nearest shuttle stop; many are at or near hotels. Parking in Springdale and riding the shuttle is also an option, especially during the busy summer season, when the Zion parking lot fills up.

Shuttle rides inside the park now require an online reservation fee of $1. The quiet, propane-powered buses serve the most visited portions in the Zion Canyon area. Both lines run most of the year except for December (but may run during the winter holidays) and January. Shuttle operations have varied in recent years, so check the park website for the latest schedules and information. Several private shuttle services also take visitors into the park from Springdale. The round-trip fee is $30 to $40 per person, plus park admission.

CAR

Zion National Park lies east of Interstate 15 in southwestern Utah. From the interstate, head east on Highway 9. After 21 miles, you'll reach Springdale, which abuts the main entrance.

From February through November, you can drive on Zion Canyon Scenic Drive only if you have reservations at the Zion Lodge and only as far as the lodge parking lot. Otherwise, you must park your car in Springdale or at the Zion Canyon Visitor Center and take the shuttle. There are usually no car restrictions in December and January, but check ahead to confirm this. If you do visit in winter when the shuttle isn't running, you won't have to miss the informative narrated shuttle tour: just download the 30-minute narration from the park's website and listen on your own device.

The Zion Canyon Visitor Center parking lot fills up quickly. You can avoid parking heartburn by leaving your car in Springdale and riding the shuttle to the park entrance. Shuttles are accessible for people with disabilities and have plenty of room for gear. Consult the print park guide or check online at ⊕ www.nps.gov/zion/plan-yourvisit/shuttle-system.htm for the town shuttle schedule.

In the north part of the park, you'll need a car to visit the Kolob Canyon area. You'll also need one to drive the breathtaking Zion–Mt. Carmel Highway (regardless of time of year). Notably, the milelong tunnel has size restrictions and escort requirements for RVs; check the park website prior to your arrival.

Just outside the park in nearby Springdale, you can fuel up, get your tires and oil changed, and have auto repairs done.

Taking the park shuttle is a relaxing way to enjoy Zion Canyon views.

Inspiration

Towers of Stone, by J. L. Crawford, summarizes the essence of Zion National Park, its landscape, plants, animals, and human history.

A Zion Canyon Reader, edited by Nathan Waite and Reid L. Neilson, is a collection of short essays both historical and recent that cover the region's exploration and development, unique features, and personal meaning to the writers. It includes works by John Wesley Powell, Clarence Dutton, Everett Ruess, Edward Abbey, Wallace Stegner, and Juanita Brooks, whose own books provide further inspiration.

Zion, by Tamra Orr, is a great introduction to the park for elementary-school kids. Part of a series titled "A True Book: National Parks," it covers the park's history, geology, scenery, plants, and animals. Get the companion books on Bryce and the Grand Canyon if your family plans to visit those parks, too.

Zion National Park: Sanctuary in the Desert, by Nicky Leach, provides a photographic overview and a narrative journey through the park. Published by the Zion Natl Park Forever Project (☎ *800/635–3959* ⊕ *www.zionpark.org*), this book and others are available at the organization's online store. It also has three stores at the park.

Park Essentials

ACCESSIBILITY

Both visitor centers, all shuttle buses, and Zion Lodge are fully accessible to people in wheelchairs. Several campsites (A24 and A25 at Watchman Campground and 103, 114, and 115 at South Campground) are reserved for people with disabilities, and two trails—Riverside Walk and Pa'rus Trail—are accessible with some assistance.

PARK FEES AND PERMITS

Entrance to Zion National Park costs $35 per vehicle for a seven-day pass. People entering on foot or by bicycle pay $20 per person for a seven-day pass; those on motorcycle pay $30.

Permits are required for backcountry camping and overnight hikes. Depending on which parts of the trails you intend to explore, you'll need a special permit for the Narrows and Kolob Creek or the Subway slot canyon. Climbing and canyoneering parties need a permit before using technical equipment.

Zion National Park limits the total number of overnight and canyoneering permits issued per day and has a reservation system, with most of the permits now issued in an online lottery to apportion them fairly. Permits for the Subway, Mystery Canyon, the Narrows through-hikes, and the West Rim are in short supply during high season. The maximum size of a group hiking into the backcountry is 12 people. Permits (available at the visitor centers) cost $15 for one or two people; $20 for three to seven; and $25 for eight or more.

PARK HOURS

The park, open daily year-round, 24 hours a day, is in the Mountain Time Zone.

CELL PHONE RECEPTION

Reception is good in Springdale but spotty in the park. Public telephones can be found at the Zion Canyon Visitor Center, Zion Lodge, and the Zion Human History Museum.

Hotels

Zion Lodge is rustic, designed in 1920s-period style, and comfortable. Most lodging is located outside the park. Springdale has dozens of options, from quaint bed-and-breakfasts to modest motels to chain hotels with riverside rooms. Farther west you'll find still more choices (and usually better values) in Hurricane and

St. George. To the east and north, you'll find a smaller number of hotels and motels, from Kanab up to Panguitch, both of which are good bases if you're continuing on to Bryce or, in the case of Kanab, the Grand Canyon.

Restaurants

Only one full-service restaurant (at the famed Zion Lodge) operates within the park, but in Springdale, just outside the South Entrance, you'll find a growing number of both casual and sophisticated eateries. To the east, there are a handful of options within an hour's drive.

Hotel and restaurant reviews have been shortened. For full information, visit Fodors.com. Restaurant prices are the average cost of a main course at dinner, or if dinner is not served, at lunch. Hotel prices are the lowest cost of a standard double room in high season.

What It Costs			
$	$$	$$$	$$$$
RESTAURANTS			
under $16	$16–$22	$23–$30	over $30
HOTELS			
under $125	$125–$175	$176–$225	over $225

Tours

★ Ranger-Led Hikes
TOUR—SIGHT | FAMILY | In summer, daily guided hikes along the 1.7-mile Pa'rus Trail provide an overview of the park's geology and natural and other history. Groups meet at 2 pm at the Zion Canyon Visitor Center. Wear sturdy footgear and bring a hat, sunglasses, sunscreen, and water. Wheelchairs are welcome on this paved trail but may need assistance. ⊠ *Zion Canyon Visitor Center, Zion National Park* ⊕ *www.nps.gov/zion/planyourvisit/ranger-led-activities.htm* ⊠ *Free.*

★ Ride with a Ranger Shuttle Tours
TOUR—SIGHT | FAMILY | Once a day, from Memorial Day through September, rangers conduct shuttle tours of points of interest along Zion Canyon Scenic Drive. In addition to learning about the

canyon's geology, ecology, and history, you'll be treated to some great photo-ops. The two-hour tour takes place in the morning and departs from the Zion Canyon Visitor Center. Make reservations in person at the visitor center up to three days in advance for up to eight people in your group. ⊠ *Zion Canyon Visitor Center, Zion National Park* ⊕ *www.nps.gov/zion/planyourvisit/ranger-led-activities.htm* 🖼 *Free* ☉ *Closed Oct.–late May.*

Visitor Information

PARK CONTACT INFORMATION Zion National Park. ⊠ *Hwy. 9, Springdale* ☎ *435/772–3256* ⊕ *www.nps.gov/zion.*

Zion Canyon

The park's main visitor center is at the South Entrance, just outside of Springdale.

The verdant sanctuary of Zion Canyon, a 6-mile oasis cut by the Virgin River, is all that some visitors need to see in one of the West's most-visited national parks. There's no denying the beauty and scale of the solid rock cliffs that dwarf the stream-fed valley below. But with a little effort and a little more time, explorations above and beyond the canyon will unlock the vast riches of this national park. Landscapes range from lava to forest to slick rock, each supporting its unique ecosystem, with wildlife from elk to songbirds and a rainbow-hue variety of flowers contrasting boldly with the surrounding desert.

As a driving destination, the park rewards visitors with three unique scenic passages. From I–15 near Cedar City, you can view the famous red cliffs and finger canyons. If you take Kolob Terrace Road to the center of the park, you'll find a remote series of trailheads that are ideal for exploring the high-desert plateau. But most drivers will relish the southern region of the park—from the principal canyon area (portions of which are closed to cars in summer) to the milelong tunnel to the moonlike eastern portion.

Similar to most national parks, however, the joy and wonder of Zion will only reveal themselves once you depart your vehicle. Short trails reward canyon visitors with incredible views, plus the sights and sounds of small animals and birds in their natural habitat. Experience the crisp, clear Virgin River carrying water that has taken thousands of years to seep through the surrounding stone. Measure 60 million geological years in the layers of rock descending down from the West Temple, 4,000 feet above you on the canyon floor. And if you find yourself here on a crisp summer night, take in one of the broadest spectrums of stars visible in North America.

 Sights

GEOLOGICAL LANDMARKS

★ The Narrows

NATURE SITE | This sinuous, 16-mile crack in the earth where the Virgin River flows over gravel and boulders is one of the world's most stunning gorges. If you hike through it, you'll find yourself surrounded—sometimes nearly boxed in—by smooth walls stretching high into the heavens. Plan to get wet, and beware that flash floods can occur here, especially in spring and summer. Check on the weather before you enter. ⊠ *Zion National Park* ⊹ *Begins at Riverside Walk.*

HISTORIC SIGHTS

Zion Human History Museum

MUSEUM | This informative museum tells the park's story from the perspective of its human inhabitants, among them Ancestral Puebloans and early Mormon settlers. Permanent exhibits illustrate how humans have dealt with wildlife, plants, and natural forces. Temporary exhibits have touched on everything from vintage park-employee photography to the history of Union Pacific Railroad hotels. Don't miss the incredible view of Towers of the Virgin from the back patio. ⊠ *Zion Canyon Scenic Dr., ½ mile north of south entrance, Zion National Park* ☎ *435/772–3256* ⊕ *www.nps.gov/zion* 🖼 *Free.*

★ Zion Lodge

HISTORIC SITE | Architect Gilbert Stanley Underwood, responsible for many noteworthy national park lodges, designed the original Zion Lodge, which opened in the 1920s but was destroyed by fire four decades later. In 1990, it was restored to its original rustic style, in some cases down to the very paint color. Natural beauty is on display inside and out, from the lobby's rock columns and exposed wood to the cottonwoods shading the sprawling lawn. The main building includes a gift shop, an upscale restaurant, and an outdoor café with a large patio and beer garden. The lodge has received numerous awards for its eco-friendly practices. Amenities include bike rentals, open-air narrated tram rides, and an electric-vehicle charging station. ⊠ *Zion Canyon Scenic Dr., Zion National Park* ☎ *435/772–7700* ⊕ *www.zionlodge.com.*

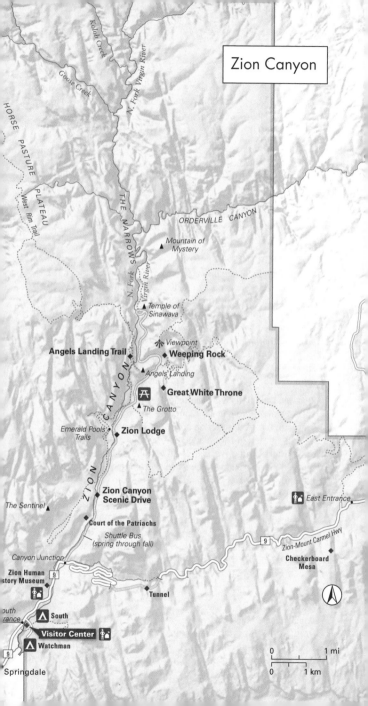

PICNIC AREAS

The Grotto

LOCAL INTEREST | **FAMILY** | Get your food to go at Zion Lodge, take a short walk to this scenic retreat, and dine beneath a shady oak. Amenities include drinking water, picnic tables, and restrooms, but there are no fire grates. A trail from here leads to the Emerald Pools. ⊠ *Off Zion Canyon Scenic Dr., at Grotto, Zion National Park.*

Zion Nature Center

LOCAL INTEREST | **FAMILY** | In summer, rangers present family programs at this center next to South Campground. There's a nice picnic area where you can feed your kids. When the center is closed, use the restrooms at the campground. ⊠ *Zion National Park ✛ Near entrance to South Campground, ½ mile north of south entrance.*

SCENIC DRIVES

★ Zion Canyon Scenic Drive

SCENIC DRIVE | Vividly colored cliffs tower 2,000 feet above the road that meanders north from Springdale along the floor of Zion Canyon. As you roll through the narrow, steep canyon, you'll pass the Court of the Patriarchs, the Sentinel, and the Great White Throne, among other imposing rock formations. From February through November, unless you're staying at the lodge, Zion Canyon Scenic Drive is accessed only by park shuttle. You can drive it yourself at other times. ⊠ *Off Hwy. 9, Zion National Park.*

Zion–Mt. Carmel Highway and Tunnels

SCENIC DRIVE | Two narrow tunnels as old as the park itself lie between the east entrance and Zion Canyon on this breathtaking 12-mile stretch of Highway 9. One was once the longest manmade tunnel in the world. As you travel the (1.1-mile) passage through solid rock, five arched portals along one side provide fleeting glimpses of cliffs and canyons. When you emerge you'll find that the landscape has changed dramatically. Large vehicles require traffic control and a $15 permit, available at the park entrance, and have restricted hours of travel. This includes nearly all RVs, trailers, dual-wheel trucks, and campers. The Canyon Overlook Trail starts from a parking area between the tunnels. ⊠ *Hwy. 9, 5 miles east of Canyon Junction, Zion National Park* ⊕ *www.nps.gov/zion/planyourvisit/the-zion-mount-carmel-tunnel. htm.*

SCENIC STOPS

Checkerboard Mesa

NATURE SITE | It's well worth stopping at the pull-out 1 mile west of Zion's east entrance to observe the distinctive waffle patterns on this huge white mound of sandstone. The stunning crosshatch

effect visible today is the result of eons of freeze-and-thaw cycles that caused vertical fractures, combined with erosion that produced horizontal bedding planes. ⊠ *Zion–Mt. Carmel Hwy., Zion National Park.*

Court of the Patriarchs

NATURE SITE | This trio of peaks bears the names of, from left to right, Abraham, Isaac, and Jacob. Mount Moroni is the reddish peak on the far right that partially blocks the view of Jacob. Hike the trail that leaves from the Court of the Patriarchs Viewpoint, 1½ miles north of Canyon Junction, to get a much better view of the sandstone prophets. ⊠ *Zion Canyon Scenic Dr., Zion National Park.*

Crawford Arch

VIEWPOINT | From the north end of the parking lot at the Zion Human History Museum, look for a display pointing out an arch high on the western slope of the opposing hill. Crawford Arch is just to the right of a saddle slope in the ridge—an easy one to view if you're keeping a "collection" of arches seen or visited in Utah. ⊠ *Zion Canyon Scenic Dr., Zion Canyon, Zion National Park* ⊕ *About 1 mile north of the park entrance.*

Great White Throne

NATURE SITE | Dominating the Grotto picnic area near Zion Lodge, this massive Navajo sandstone peak juts 2,000 feet above the valley floor. The popular formation lies about 3 miles north of Canyon Junction. ⊠ *Zion Canyon Scenic Dr., Zion National Park.*

Weeping Rock

NATURE SITE | Surface water from the rim of Echo Canyon spends several thousand years seeping down through the porous sandstone before exiting at this picturesque alcove 4½ miles north of Canyon Junction. A paved walkway climbs ¼ mile to this flowing rock face where wildflowers and delicate ferns grow. In fall, the maples and cottonwoods burst with color, and lizards point the way down the path, which is too steep for wheelchairs or strollers. A major rockslide closed the Weeping Rock Trail in summer 2019; check with the visitor center to see if it has reopened. ⊠ *Zion Canyon Scenic Dr., Zion National Park.*

TRAILS

★ Angels Landing Trail

TRAIL | As much a trial as a trail, this path beneath the Great White Throne, which you access from the Lower West Rim Trail, is one of the park's most challenging hikes. Early on, you work your way through Walter's Wiggles, a series of 21 switchbacks built out of sandstone blocks. From there you traverse sheer cliffs that have chains bolted into the rock face to serve as handrails in some (but not all) places. In spite of its hair-raising nature, this trail is popular. Allow 2½ hours round trip if you stop at Scout's Lookout (2 miles), and 4 hours if you keep going to where the angels (and birds of prey) play. The trail is 5 miles round trip and is not appropriate for children or those who are uneasy about heights. *Difficult.* ⊠ *Zion National Park* ✛ *Trailhead: off Zion Canyon Scenic Dr. at the Grotto.*

★ Canyon Overlook Trail

TRAIL | FAMILY | The parking area just east of Zion–Mt. Carmel Tunnel leads to this popular trail, which is about 1 mile round trip and takes about an hour to finish. From the breathtaking overlook at the trail's end, you can see the West and East temples, the Towers of the Virgin, the Streaked Wall, and other Zion Canyon cliffs and peaks. The elevation change is 160 feet. There's no shuttle to this trail, and the parking area often fills up—try to come very early or late in the day to avoid crowds. *Moderate.* ⊠ *Zion National Park* ✛ *Trailhead: off Hwy. 9 just east of Zion–Mt. Carmel Tunnel.*

Emerald Pools Trail

TRAIL | FAMILY | Multiple waterfalls cascade (or drip, in dry weather) into algae-filled pools along this trail, about 3 miles north of Canyon Junction. The path leading to the lower pool is paved and appropriate for strollers and wheelchairs. If you've got any energy left, keep going past the lower pool. The ¼ mile from there to the middle pool becomes rocky and somewhat steep but offers increasingly scenic views. A less crowded and exceptionally enjoyable return route follows the Kayenta Trail, connecting to the Grotto Trail. Allow 50 minutes for the 1¼-mile round-trip hike to the lower pool, and an hour more each round trip to the middle (2 miles) and upper pools (3 miles). *Lower, easy. Upper, moderate.* ⊠ *Zion National Park* ✛ *Trailhead: off Zion Canyon Scenic Dr., at Zion Lodge or the Grotto.*

Grotto Trail

TRAIL | FAMILY | This flat trail takes you from Zion Lodge, about 3 miles north of Canyon Junction, to the Grotto picnic area, traveling for the most part along the park road. Allow 20 minutes or less for the walk along the ½-mile trail. If you are up for a longer hike and have two or three hours, connect with the Kayenta Trail after you cross the footbridge, and head for the Emerald Pools. You will begin gaining elevation, and it's a steady, steep climb to the pools, which you will begin to see after about 1 mile. *Easy.* ⊠ *Zion National Park* ✛ *Trailhead: off Zion Canyon Scenic Dr. at the Grotto.*

Did You Know?

Zion's formations have up to nine layers (try counting them at vistas like this one!) of sedimentary rock deposited between 100 and 270 million years ago.

Hidden Canyon Trail

TRAIL | This steep, 2-mile round-trip hike takes you up 850 feet in elevation. Not too crowded, the trail is paved all the way to Hidden Canyon. Allow about three hours for the round-trip hike. A massive rockfall in summer 2019 resulted in the closure of this trail—check with the visitor center for updates. *Moderate–Difficult.* ⊠ *Zion National Park* ✛ *Trailhead: off Zion Canyon Scenic Dr. at Weeping Rock.*

★ The Narrows Trail

TRAIL | After leaving the paved ease of the Gateway to the Narrows trail behind, walk on the riverbed itself. You'll find a pebbly shingle or dry sandbar path, but when the walls of the canyon close in, you'll be forced into the chilly waters of the Virgin River. A walking stick and good shoes are a must. Be prepared to swim, as chest-deep holes may occur even when water levels are low. Check with park rangers about the likelihood of flash floods. A day trip up the lower section of the Narrows is 6 miles one way to the turnaround point. Allow at least five hours round trip. *Difficult.* ⊠ *Zion National Park* ✛ *Trailhead: off Zion Canyon Scenic Dr., at the end of Riverside Walk.*

The Narrows Trail (From the Top)

TRAIL | "From the Top" means shuttling out to Chamberlain Ranch northeast of the park and following the canyon for 16 miles to the Temple of Sinawava. It can be done as a day hike, but most hikers stop at one of 12 backcountry campsites in the park. You'll have to rappel down 12-foot waterfalls, wander through miles of river, and explore multiple side canyons. On the plus side, it's all downhill! Ropes and rappelling equipment are required, as are backcountry permits. Several local outfitters offer shuttle service to Chamberlain Ranch; if you're driving yourself, turn left after you cross the Virgin River and drive ¼ mile to Chamberlain Ranch. Drive ½ mile farther and park just before the road crosses the river. Follow this road for 3 miles on foot and enter the river when the road ends. *Difficult.* ⊠ *Chamberlain Ranch, Zion National Park* ✛ *Approx. 18 miles north of Rte. 9 on the park's east side* ⊕ *www.nps.gov/zion/planyourvisit/narrowstopdown.htm.*

Observation Point Trail

TRAIL | More than one park ranger says this is their favorite hike. Three miles longer than Angels Landing and with 50% more vertical elevation gain, this strenuous hike is too much for many—meaning you'll have much more solitude. The 8-mile, half-day (five-hour) round-trip trek takes you past rocks bursting with moisture between towering cliffs and rewards you with a view down into Big Bend and Zion Canyon. You can even look *down* on Angels

Landing. Note: A major rockfall closed this trail in 2019; check with the visitor center for its current status. *Difficult.* ⊠ *Zion Canyon Scenic Dr., Zion Canyon, Zion National Park* ✛ *4 miles north of Canyon Junction.*

Orderville Canyon

TRAIL | This 12-mile, one-way hike begins east of the park and terminates in the Narrows of the Virgin River about 2 miles north of the Temple of Sinawava. More than half of the trek is outside park boundaries. Access the canyon via a dirt road (North Fork Road) approximately 4 miles east of Zion's East Entrance on Route 9. Similar to the Narrows, you walk in the river and along its rocky shoreline through increasingly steep, narrow, and waterlogged terrain. Ropes and rappelling equipment are required, as are canyoneering permits (which must be reserved in advance from the National Park Service's website). *Difficult.* ⊠ *Zion National Park* ⊕ *www.nps.gov/zion/.*

Pa'rus Trail

TRAIL | **FAMILY** | An approximately 1¾-mile, relatively flat, paved walking and biking path, Pa'rus parallels and occasionally crosses the Virgin River. Starting at South Campground, ½ mile north of the South Entrance, the walk proceeds north along the river to the beginning of Zion Canyon Scenic Drive. Along the way you'll take in great views of the Watchman, the Sentinel, the East and West temples, and the Towers of the Virgin. Leashed dogs are allowed on this trail. Wheelchair users may need assistance. *Easy.* ⊠ *Zion National Park* ✛ *Trailhead: at Canyon Junction.*

Riverside Walk

TRAIL | **FAMILY** | This 2.2-mile round-trip hike shadows the Virgin River. In spring, wildflowers bloom on the opposite canyon wall in lovely hanging gardens. The trail, which begins 6½ miles north of Canyon Junction at the end of Zion Canyon Scenic Drive, is the park's most visited, so be prepared for crowds in high season. Riverside Walk is paved and suitable for strollers and wheelchairs, though some wheelchair users may need assistance. Round trip it takes about 90 minutes. At the end, the much more challenging Narrows Trail begins. *Easy.* ⊠ *Zion National Park* ✛ *Trailhead: off Zion Canyon Scenic Dr. at the Temple of Sinawava.*

Watchman Trail

TRAIL | For a dramatic view of Springdale and a look at lower Zion Creek Canyon and Towers of the Virgin, this strenuous hike begins on a service road east of Watchman Campground. Some springs seep out of the sandstone, nourishing the hanging gardens and attracting wildlife. There are a few sheer cliff edges, so supervise children carefully. Plan on two hours for this 3.3-mile round-trip

Spend an hour or half a day exploring the lower, middle, and/or upper Emerald Pools.

hike that has a 368-foot elevation change. *Moderate.* ✉ *Zion National Park* ✛ *Trailhead: at Zion Canyon Visitor Center.*

Weeping Rock Trail

TRAIL | FAMILY | A half-mile round-trip, this is definitely a kid-friendly trail. Hop off the bus three stops from the north end of the park. The well-marked trail is shaded and has a steady incline that leads to steps as you approach the alcove. Although much of the trail is paved, the steepness and irregularity may make it difficult for strollers and wheelchairs. Amaze your kids when you tell them the water trickling down on them has taken more than 1,000 years to seep down and through Echo Canyon. In 2019, the trail was closed after it was damaged by a massive rockfall; check with the visitor center about its current status. *Easy.* ✉ *Zion Canyon Scenic Dr., Zion Canyon, Zion National Park* ✛ *4 miles north of Canyon Junction.*

VISITOR CENTERS

Zion Canyon Visitor Center

INFO CENTER | Learn about the area's geology, flora, and fauna at an outdoor exhibit next to a gurgling stream. Inside, a large shop sells everything from field guides to souvenirs. Zion Canyon shuttle buses leave regularly from the center and make several stops along the canyon's beautiful Scenic Drive; ranger-guided shuttle tours depart once a day from Memorial Day to late September. ✉ *Zion Park Blvd. at south entrance, Springdale* ☎ *435/772–3256* ⊕ *www.nps.gov/zion.*

Extraordinary canyon views are the reward for hiking the 8-mile round-trip Observation Point Trail.

🍴 Restaurants

Castle Dome Café & Snack Bar

$ | CAFÉ | Next to the shuttle stop at Zion Lodge, this small, convenient, fast-food restaurant has a lovely shaded patio. You can grab a banana, burger, smoothie, or salad to go, order local brews from the Beer Garden cart, or enjoy a dish of ice cream while soaking up the views of the surrounding geological formations. **Known for:** quick bites; gorgeous views; nice beer selection. ⑤ *Average main: $6* ⊠ *Zion Lodge, Zion Canyon Scenic Dr., Zion National Park* 🕾 *435/772–7700* ⊕ *www.zionlodge.com/dining/castle-dome-cafe* ☉ *Closed Dec.–Feb.*

Red Rock Grill

$$ | AMERICAN | The dinner fare at this restaurant in Zion Lodge includes steaks, seafood, and Western specialties, such as pecan-encrusted trout and jalapeño-topped bison cheeseburgers; salads, sandwiches, and hearty burgers are lunch highlights; and, for breakfast, you can partake of the plentiful buffet or order off the menu. Photos showcasing the surrounding landscape adorn the walls of the spacious dining room; enormous windows and a large patio take in the actual landscape. **Known for:** dinner reservations necessary in summer; astounding views inside and out; only full-service restaurant in the park. ⑤ *Average main: $19* ⊠ *Zion Lodge, Zion Canyon Scenic Dr., Zion National Park* 🕾 *435/772–7760* ⊕ *www.zionlodge.com/dining/red-rock-grill.*

Hotels

★ Zion Lodge

$$$$ | **HOTEL** | For a dramatic location inside the park, you'd be hard-pressed to improve on a stay at the historic Zion Lodge: the canyon's jaw-dropping beauty surrounds you, access to trailheads is easy, and guests can drive their cars on the lower half of Zion Park Scenic Drive year-round. **Pros:** handsome hotel in the tradition of historic park properties; incredible views; bike rentals on-site. **Cons:** pathways are dimly lit (bring a flashlight); spotty Wi-Fi, poor cell service; books up months ahead. ⑤ *Rooms from: $229* ⊠ *Zion Canyon Scenic Dr., Zion National Park* ☎ *888/297–2757 reservations only, 435/772–7700* ⊕ *www.zionlodge.com* ⇱ *122 rooms* ❏ *No meals.*

Shopping

Zion Canyon Visitor Center Store

GIFTS/SOUVENIRS | The comprehensive shop at the park's main visitor center sells maps and travel books, puzzles, jewelry, apparel, posters, Native American items, DVDs, and gear, such as water bottles. The Zion Natl Park Forever Project operates the store. ⊠ *South Entrance, Zion National Park* ☎ *435/772–3264* ⊕ *www.zionpark.org.*

Zion Lodge Gift Shop

GIFTS/SOUVENIRS | The lodge's gift shop has everything from nature books and hiking gear to Native American jewelry and leather goods. ⊠ *Zion Canyon Scenic Dr., 3¼ miles north of Canyon Junction, Zion National Park* ☎ *435/772–7700.*

Kolob Canyons

Kolob Canyons is 38 miles northwest of Springdale via I–15 and Kolob Terrace Rd.

Often overlooked by park visitors, Kolob Canyons and Kolob Terrace offer windows into an entirely different habitat than that of Zion Canyon. About 45 minutes from Springdale, the Kolob Canyons section showcases the red rocks of the park's northwest corner. It's accessible from I–15 at Exit 40, and nothing in the appearance of the unassuming visitor center here hints at the lush red canyons that cut into the mountains behind it. The entire 5-mile road is within park boundaries, with two trailheads offering day hikes and one trailhead leading into the vast backcountry.

Kolob Terrace Road runs to lava fields, a reservoir, and a free (yes, free!) campground in the heart of the park's backcountry. Unlike Kolob Canyons Road, much of this road is outside park boundaries, hopscotching through Bureau of Land Management and private land. Look for evidence of prehistoric volcanic activity, with black rock prevailing here rather than the red clay and white sandstone that characterizes much of the rest of the park. There are several noteworthy peaks to see, several trailheads through which to access the backcountry, and, finally, Kolob Reservoir—a victim of too many dry years recently.

Sights

PICNIC AREAS

Kolob Canyons Viewpoint

LOCAL INTEREST | FAMILY | Nearly 100% of travelers along Interstate 15 from Las Vegas to Salt Lake overlook this short drive a few hundred yards from the highway. The reward is a beautiful view of Kolob's "finger" canyons from about six picnic tables spread out beneath the trees. The parking lot has plenty of space, a pit toilet, and an overlook with a display pointing out canyon features. Restrooms and drinking water are available 5 miles away at the Kolob Canyons Visitor Center. ⊠ *Zion National Park* ✛ *On Timber Creek Trail at the end of Kolob Canyons Rd.*

SCENIC DRIVES

Kolob Canyons Road

SCENIC DRIVE | Kolob Canyons Road is a 5-mile immersion into red rock canyons that extend east-to-west along three forks of Taylor Creek and La Verkin Creek. The beauty starts modestly at the junction with Interstate 15, but as you move along this 5-mile road, the red walls of the Kolob finger canyons rise suddenly and spectacularly. With the crowds left behind at Zion Canyon, this drive offers the chance to take in incredible vistas at your leisure. Trails include the short but rugged Middle Fork of Taylor Creek Trail, which passes two 1930s homestead cabins, culminating 2¾ miles later in the Double Arch Alcove. At the end of the drive, take the short hike to the Kolob Canyons Viewpoint to see Nagunt Mesa, Shuntavi Butte, and Gregory Butte, each rising to nearly 8,000 feet above sea level. During heavy snowfall Kolob Canyons Road may be closed. ⊠ *I–15, Exit 40, Zion National Park.*

Kolob Terrace Road

SCENIC DRIVE | Hundreds of miles of scenic desert roads criss-cross the Southwest, and Kolob Terrace Road will remind you of many of them. Sprawling as much as 4,000 feet above the floor of Zion Canyon, and without the benefit of the canyon's breezes

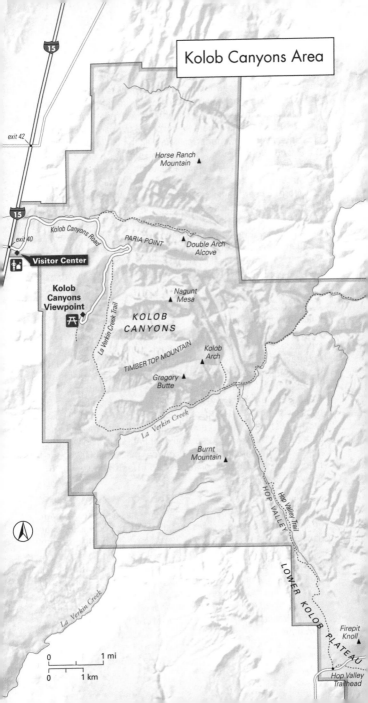

Kolob Canyons Area

exit 42

15

exit 40

Kolob Canyons Road

Visitor Center

Kolob
Canyons
Viewpoint

La Verkin Creek Trail

PARIA POINT

Horse Ranch
Mountain ▲

Double Arch
Alcove ▲

Nagunt
Mesa ▲

KOLOB
CANYONS

TIMBER TOP MOUNTAIN

Kolob
Arch ▲

Gregory
Butte ▲

La Verkin Creek

Burnt
Mountain ▲

HOP VALLEY

Hop Valley Trail

LOWER KOLOB PLATEAU

La Verkin Creek

Firepit
Knoll ▲

Hop Valley
Trailhead

0   1 mi

0   1 km

and shade, the landscape along it is arid—browns and grays and ambers—but not without rugged beauty. The 21-mile stretch begins 15 miles west of Springdale at Virgin and winds north. As you travel along, peaks and knolls emerge from the high plateau, birds circle overhead, and you might not see more than a half-dozen cars. The drive meanders in and out of the park boundaries, crossing several important trailheads, all the while overlooking the cliffs of North Creek. A popular day-use trail (permit required) leads past fossilized dinosaur tracks to the Subway, a stretch of the stream where the walls of the slot canyon close in so tightly as to form a near tunnel. Farther along the road is the Wildcat Canyon trailhead, which connects to the path overlooking the North Guardian Angel. The road terminates at the Kolob Reservoir, beneath 8,933-foot Kolob Peak. Although paved, this narrow, twisting road is not recommended for RVs. Because of limited winter plowing, the road is closed from November or December through April or May. ⊠ *Zion National Park* ✛ *Begins in Virgin at Hwy. 9.*

SCENIC STOPS

Kolob Canyons Viewpoint

VIEWPOINT | At the end of Kolob Canyons Road, pause for a picnic and stare down the tips of the "finger" canyons to the east. Shuntavi Butte juts out from Timber Top Mountain (8,075 feet) to the southeast. Stroll the easy, 30-minute, 1-mile round-trip Timber Creek Overlook Trail, which takes in the contours of the creek and the spot where intrepid hikers go to view what is possibly the country's largest freestanding natural arch—Kolob Arch. Reaching it (via La Verkin Creek Trail) is a 14-mile round-trip undertaking, however, so hold off on it until you've consulted with the backcountry ranger at the visitor center. ⊠ *Kolob Canyons Rd., Kolob Canyons, Zion National Park* ✛ *5 miles southwest of Kolob Canyons Entrance.*

Lava Point

VIEWPOINT | Infrequently visited, this area has a primitive campground and two nearby reservoirs that offer the only significant fishing opportunities in the park. Lava Point Overlook, one of the park's highest viewpoints, provides vistas of Zion Canyon from the north. The higher elevation here makes it much cooler than the Zion Canyon area. Park visitors looking for a respite from crowds and heat find the campground a nice change of pace, though the six sites fill up quickly and are only open May through September. ⊠ *Zion National Park* ✛ *Kolob Terrace Rd. to Lava Point Rd., then turn right.*

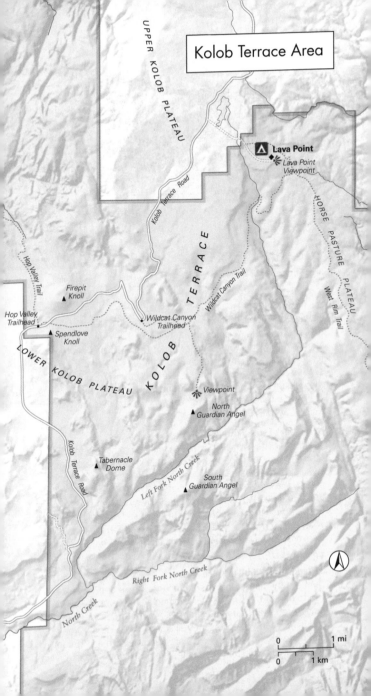

Kolob Terrace Area

UPPER KOLOB PLATEAU

⛺ Lava Point
❖🎇 Lava Point Viewpoint

Kolob Terrace Road

HORSE PASTURE PLATEAU

Hop Valley Trail

KOLOB TERRACE

Wildcat Canyon Trail

West Rim Trail

▲ Firepit Knoll

Hop Valley Trailhead

● Wildcat Canyon Trailhead

▲ Spendlove Knoll

LOWER KOLOB PLATEAU

KOLOB

🎇 Viewpoint

▲ North Guardian Angel

Kolob Terrace Road

▲ Tabernacle Dome

South ▲ Guardian Angel

Left Fork North Creek

Right Fork North Creek

North Creek

0   1 mi
0   1 km

Rugged, arid, and beautiful red-rock landscapes await on the 21-mile Kolob Terrace Road.

Lee Pass

VIEWPOINT | The hairpin turn on Kolob Canyons Road offers you a roadside pullout and an opportunity to glimpse deep into the canyon carved by the South Fork of Taylor Creek. This is the trailhead for the Kolob Arch hike, which also connects you to the main section of Zion National Park via the backcountry. Don't head into the wilderness without a backcountry permit. ⊠ *Kolob Canyons Rd., Kolob Canyons, Zion National Park* ✛ *3 miles southwest of Kolob Canyons Entrance.*

North Creek Left Fork Trailhead

VIEWPOINT | The trailhead for hikers wishing to hike to the Subway "from the bottom up," this parking area is adjacent to sharp, black lava fields interspersed with hearty cacti. Follow the trail about 1 mile to the cliff's edge to see where Subway hikers descend to the river and head upstream to the Subway. Watch birds circle in front of the cliff face to the north. Don't head down the steep trail without a permit from park rangers. ⊠ *Kolob Terrace Rd., Kolob Canyons, Zion National Park* ✛ *7 miles north of Rte. 9.*

TRAILS

La Verkin Creek Trail to Kolob Arch

TRAIL | In the park's northwest corner, a 7-mile one-way hike leads you to one of the largest freestanding arches ever discovered. Kolob Arch spans nearly the length of a football field (287 feet) and is reached via a pleasant trail alongside La Verkin Creek and beneath the vivid red cliffs of Shuntavi Butte and Timber Top Mountain. Multiple campsites are available to make this an overnight itinerary (a permit is required for an overnight stay). Connect to the Hop Valley Trail to head into the main portion of Zion National Park. *Difficult.* ✉ *Lee Pass Trailhead, Kolob Canyons Rd., Kolob Canyons, Zion National Park* ✛ *Approx. 3 miles east of Kolob Canyons Visitor Center* ⊕ *www.nps.gov/zion/planyourvisit/ traildescriptions.htm.*

The Subway Bottom-Up Trail

TRAIL | The Left Fork of North Creek is one of Zion's most awe-inspiring mapped features (the locals, though, are hiding some from outsiders). Determined hikers can manage its 9-mile round-trip trek from "the bottom up" in a day (plan on 6 to 10 hours) but will need a permit. (A limited number are available on 24 hours' notice; arrive at the Zion Visitor Center by 7 am if you hope to get one.) This journey begins with a milelong hike across the black-lava field remnants of an ancient volcanic eruption. Then you must negotiate a steep descent to the riverbed and head upstream. Highlights include intersections with several smaller canyon streams and a 30-foot trailside slab of dinosaur prints (on the north side of the creek just past the second connecting canyon—ask a ranger at the Kolob Canyons Visitor Center to show you on a map). Mostly, though, you have the pristine serenity of the river carving slick rock and then the Subway itself. You may have to climb a watery incline or two, as the river moistens the entire creek bed, but the Subway will be worth it. Think of a subway tunnel with a river of water emanating from it instead of a train—enter at your own risk, though. *Difficult.* ✉ *Kolob Terrace Rd., Kolob Canyons, Zion National Park* ✛ *Approx. 7 miles north of Rte. 9* ⊕ *www.nps.gov/ zion/planyourvisit/subway-bottom-up.htm.*

The Subway Top-Down Trail

TRAIL | Start at the Wildcat Canyon Trailhead, near Lava Point, and emerge at the Left Fork trailhead, both along Kolob Terrace Road. The 9.5-mile trek requires that you carry at least 60 feet of rope; swim through deep, debris-filled pools (wetsuits recommended); and have extensive route-finding experience. The reward is a subway tunnel–like rock formation that has been carved by the river. Descend from the arid plateau and emerge in a lush riverbed lined with trees and impossibly high cliffs. Other highlights include a 30-foot slab of dinosaur tracks, numerous side canyons, and the volcanic rock fields at Left Fork trailhead. A permit is required and generally must be reserved well in advance (limited permits are available by lottery a week or less before desired date and very occasionally on a walk-in basis). The trek must be completed the same day. First-timers are encouraged to travel with someone who has hiked this route to the Subway before. *Difficult.* ✉ *Wildcat Canyon Trailhead, Kolob Terrace Rd., Kolob Canyons, Zion*

National Park ✛ *17 miles north of Rte. 9* ⊕ *www.nps.gov/zion/ planyourvisit/thesubway.htm.*

Taylor Creek Trail

TRAIL | This trail in the Kolob Canyons area descends parallel to Taylor Creek, sometimes crossing it, sometimes shortcutting benches beside it. The historic Larson Cabin precedes the entrance to the canyon of the Middle Fork, where the trail becomes rougher. After the old Fife Cabin, the canyon bends to the right into Double Arch Alcove, a large, colorful grotto with a high blind arch (or arch "embryo") towering above. To Double Arch it's 2½ miles one way—about four hours round trip. The elevation change is 450 feet. *Moderate.* ⊠ *Zion National Park* ✛ *Trailhead: at Kolob Canyons Rd., about 1½ miles east of Kolob Canyons Visitor Center.*

Timber Creek Overlook Trail

TRAIL | **FAMILY** | Don't miss this short hike at the end of Kolob Canyons Road. Covered with desert wildflowers in spring and early summer, it's barely a mile round-trip on a sandy, relatively exposed plateau above the surrounding valleys. Get a good look at the Kolob Canyons "skyline," including Shuntavi Butte in the shadow of 8,055-foot Timber Top Mountain. The last few hundred yards are a little rockier with a 100-foot ascent, but most children and senior citizens shouldn't have any problems with it. As with many locations in the park, this trailhead starts at more than a mile above sea level—6,250 feet. Also, the picnic area 100 yards from the trailhead offers four tables, ample shade, and a suitable spot for little ones to chase after lizards, chipmunks, squirrels, and the occasional long-eared, black-tailed jackrabbit. *Easy.* ⊠ *Kolob Canyons Rd., Zion National Park* ✛ *At the end of Kolob Canyons Rd., about 5 miles from Kolob Canyons Visitor Center* ⊕ *www.nps. gov/zion/planyourvisit/kolob-canyons-wilderness-hiking-trails.htm.*

West Rim Trail

TRAIL | Hike from Lava Point to the Grotto (about 13½ miles) along the high plateaus west of the Virgin River. Temperatures here may be 10 to 15 degrees cooler than those in Zion Canyon due to the altitude, but your exposure to the sun may be greater, so plan accordingly. Nine campsites along the way allow you to break up this hike, and some can be reserved in advance. Permits are required. *Difficult.* ⊠ *West Rim trailhead near Lava Point, Kolob Terrace Rd., Kolob Canyons, Zion National Park* ✛ *20 miles north of Rte. 9* ⊕ *www.nps.gov/zion/planyourvisit/west-rim-trail.htm.*

VISITOR CENTERS
Kolob Canyons Visitor Center
INFO CENTER | Make this your first stop as you enter this remote section of the park. There are books and maps, a small gift shop, and clean restrooms here, and rangers are on hand to answer questions about Kolob Canyons exploration. ⊠ *3752 E. Kolob Canyons Rd., Exit 40 off I–15, Zion National Park* ☎ *435/772–3256* ⊕ *www.nps.gov/zion.*

Activities

Adventure Tours

Zion Adventure Company
TOUR—SPORTS | FAMILY | Zion Aventure Company has guided, equipped, and offered advice on a wide range of of desert adventures since 1996. Countless tourists heading upstream on the Narrows carry Zion Adventure walking sticks and neoprene Aqua Sox footwear. The company offers guided hikes on park trails, including the Narrows, and shuttle service to the Narrows trailhead and a few other park locations. They have special family adventures, including rock climbing and canyoneering, as well as bike tours and rentals, multiday canyoneering experiences, rock-climbing courses, photography tours, and workshops. The friendly staff will indulge every "silly" question in their quest to get you on the trail—and home again—safely. Rental rates for Narrows gear range from $27 for footwear only to $57 for a full drysuit. Guided hikes and family rock-climbing and canyoneering adventures start at $159 per person for a half-day. All-day advanced outings are $279 per person; one-on-one guided experiences cost $499. ⊠ *36 Lion Blvd., Springdale* ☎ *435/772–1001* ⊕ *www.zionadventures.com.*

Zion Guru
TOUR—SPORTS | FAMILY | With a holistic approach to adventure, this guide service teaches canyoneering skills to beginners as young as age 5 and guides advanced tours as well. They offer half- and full-day rock-climbing and guided hikes, including into the Narrows. They also rent e-bikes and gear for the Narrows and run a shuttle service to park trailheads. Fees start at $69 for half-day e-bike rentals or $182 for half-day canyoneering adventures. ⊠ *792 Zion Park Blvd., Springdale* ☎ *435/632–0462* ⊕ *www.ziongurus.com.*

Biking

The introduction of the park shuttle has improved bicycling conditions in Zion National Park, for during the busy months, April through October, cyclists no longer share Zion Canyon Scenic Drive with thousands of cars—though two-wheelers do need to be cautious of the large buses plying the park road throughout the day. Within the park proper, bicycles are only allowed on established park roads and on the 3½-mile Pa'rus Trail, which winds along the Virgin River in Zion Canyon. You cannot ride your bicycle through the Zion–Mt. Carmel tunnels; the only way to get your bike past this stretch of the highway is to transport it by motor vehicle.

Outside the park, southern Utah is home to a booming road cycling community. Ask at any bike shop in the region for favorite routes. Mountain bikers are increasingly drawn to Gooseberry Mesa, which locals consider equal to or better than the famous Moab slickrock mountain-biking trails.

Bike Zion

BICYCLING | Here you can rent Kona and Jamis bikes and set up supported road-cycling trips and single-track and/or slickrock adventures at nearby Gooseberry Mesa. The company also rents car racks and trailers and can give you tips on the local trails. Day trips and multiday tours are available. Ask them about the best area trails if you prefer to explore on your own. Bike rentals start at $50 for a half-day; tour rates, which depend on group size, range from $131 to $170 per person. ⊠ *1458 Zion Park Blvd., Springdale* ☎ *435/772–3303* ⊕ *www.bikingzion.com.*

Zion Cycles

BICYCLING | This shop just outside the park rents bikes by the hour or longer, sells parts, and has a full-time mechanic on duty. You can pick up trail tips and other advice from the staff here. They also offer guided road-biking treks in the park and mountain-biking excursions elsewhere in southern Utah. ⊠ *868 Zion Park Blvd., Springdale* ☎ *435/772–0400* ⊕ *www.zioncycles.com* ✍ *Guided tours from $175; bike rentals from $40/day.*

Bird-Watching

Nearly 300 bird species call Zion Canyon home, and scores more pass through the park on their annual migrations. Some species, such as the white-throated swift and ospreys, thrive in the towering cliff walls. Red-tailed and Cooper's hawks are abundant. Closer to the ground you'll doubtless see the bold Steller's jay and scrub jay rustling around the pinyon thickets. The wild turkey population has boomed in recent years; some of the flock might come your way looking for a handout. Five species of hummingbirds reside in the park, with the black-chinned variety being the most common. You might spot members of four transient species as well. Climb to the top of Angel's Landing and you might glimpse a bald eagle. Two of the park's rarest species are the Mexican spotted owl and the enormous California condor. ■ TIP→ **Ask for the Zion Bird List brochure at the visitor center or download one.** ⊕ *www.nps.gov/ zion/learn/nature/birds.htm*

Camping

The two primary campgrounds within Zion National Park are family-friendly, convenient, and generally pleasant, but in the high season they do fill up fast. Don't expect solitude as both South Campground and Watchman Campground host hundreds of campers every night in high season. In midsummer, Zion's searing heat can leave the campgrounds fairly deserted in midday. Flock to the river, nearby canyons, and/or higher altitude to find some relief.

Backcountry camping in the park is an option for overnight backpackers, but make sure to get a permit at the Zion Canyon or Kolob Canyons visitor centers. The primitive Lava Point Campground has no water and is closed in winter and spring but is a rarity as a free place to stay inside the national park. Its six sites are first-come, first-served.

Outside the park, there are options to the north, east, and west. Regardless, your best bet is to reserve ahead of time whenever possible. Private campgrounds cater to families, often featuring amenities such as playgrounds, showers, picnic areas, and, in some cases, swimming pools.

Lava Point Campground. This little-known gem of a campground is within park limits but accessible by car only by driving the length of Kolob Terrace Road, which intersects Route 9 in the town of Virgin, 13.6 miles east of the park entrance. Follow Kolob Terrace Road 20 miles north, then turn right at the campground sign. The sparsely maintained road may be impassable after heavy rains. Your journey is rewarded with six peaceful, tree-shaded campsites at 7,800 feet above sea level (and thus about 10°F cooler on average than the Zion Park Visitor Center). These primitive campsites have fire pits and picnic tables but no potable water. There is no charge to camp here. The adjacent trailheads offer access to the West Rim Trail and Wildcat Canyon. ⊠ *Access road off Kolob Terrace Rd.* ☎ *435/772–3256* ⚲ *6 sites.*

South Campground. All the sites here are under big cottonwood trees that provide some relief from the summer sun. Many of the sites are suitable for either tents or RVs, although there are no hookups. The campground operates on a reservation system. ⊠ *Hwy. 9, ½ mile north of south entrance* ☎ *435/772–3256, 877/444–6777* ⊕ *www.recreation.gov* ⚲ *127 sites.*

Watchman Campground. This large campground on the Virgin River operates on a reservation system between March and November, but you do not get to choose your site. With five loops of campsites, the campground allows everyone from tent-toting hikers to RVers to rub shoulders. Loops C and D are tent-only and quieter than the RV area. Several group sites can accommodate as many as 50 people each, turning this campground into one of the rowdier places to stay. An amphitheater hosts nightly ranger talks on topics from the park's flora and fauna to tall tales and legends. Walk to the Zion Canyon Visitor Center and to the Pa'rus Trail. Sometimes you can get same-day reservations, but don't count on it. ⊠ *Access road off Zion Canyon Visitor Center parking lot* ☎ *435/772–3256, 877/444–6777* ⊕ *www.recreation.gov* ⚲ *164 sites, 95 with hookups.*

Educational Programs

CLASSES AND SEMINARS

★ Zion Natl Park Forever Project

TOUR—SIGHT | Formerly known as the Zion Natural History Association, this organization conducts in-park workshops on natural and cultural history. Topics can include edible plants, bat biology, river geology, photography, and bird-watching. Most workshops include a hike. For a glimpse of Zion's inner workings, volunteer to assist with one of their ongoing service projects. ⊠ *Zion National Park* ☎ *435/772–3264* ⊕ *www.zionpark.org* ⛁ *From $45.*

RANGER PROGRAMS

Evening Programs

TOUR—SIGHT | Held each evening May through September in Watchman Campground and at Zion Lodge, these 45-minute ranger-led talks cover geology, biology, and history. You might learn about coyote calls, the night sky, animal hideouts, or observing nature with all your senses. Slide shows and audience participation are often part of the proceedings. Check the visitor center for schedules. ⊠ *Zion National Park* ⊕ *www.nps.gov/zion/planyourvisit/ranger-led-activities.htm.*

Plants and Wildlife in Zion

Zion, which is on the Colorado Plateau and bordered by the Great Basin and Mojave Desert provinces, has over 1,000 species of plants that thrive in environments ranging from desert to hanging garden to high plateau. Look for delicate ferns and mosses; hardy cacti; and many trees, grasses, and herbs. Poison ivy, abundant here, is one species to avoid.

When car traffic is replaced by a shuttle from February through November, wildlife returns in force. Even in high season you can spot mule deer in shady glens, especially in early morning and near dusk. You'll also see lizards and wild turkeys.

Nearly 300 species of birds reside here, from tiny hummingbirds and chickadees to eagles and pelicans. Ringtail cats (similar to raccoons) prowl the park. Evening hikes may reveal foxes, though you're more likely to spot just their tracks. Although only the rare mountain lion or black bear poses a threat, give all animals plenty of space.

★ Expert Talks

TOUR—SIGHT | Informal lectures take place on the Zion Human History Museum patio. Past topics have included wildlife, geology, and the stories of early settlers. Talks usually last from 20 to 30 minutes, though some run longer. Check park bulletin boards or the visitor center for schedules. ⊠ *Zion National Park* ⊕ *www.nps. gov/zion/planyourvisit/ranger-led-activities.htm.*

Junior Ranger Program

TOUR—SIGHT | **FAMILY** | Educational activities aimed at younger visitors include the chance to earn a Junior Ranger badge. Kids do so by attending at least one nature program and completing the free *Junior Ranger Handbook,* available at visitor centers. ⊠ *Zion National Park* ⊕ *www.nps.gov/zion/learn/kidsyouth/beajuniorranger.htm.*

Fishing

The waterfalls and rough terrain of the Virgin River and its nearby creeks do not make for ideal fishing conditions. Still, fishing is allowed as long as you have a Utah State fishing license. You may catch (and keep) trout. Just outside the park, Kolob Reservoir (8,000 feet above sea level) offers decent but unspectacular trout angling. Look for the dirt road at the end of Kolob Terrace Road, about 5 miles north of Lava Point.

Only 10% of visitors make it to Kolob Canyons for views like this from Timber Creek Overlook.

Hiking

The best way to experience Zion Canyon is to walk beneath, between, and, if you can bear it (and have good balance!), along its towering cliffs. There's something for everyone, from paved and flat river strolls to precarious cliff-side scrambles. Zion also offers a vast backcountry spanning elevations from less than 4,000 feet above sea level to as high as 8,000 feet. The wild lands encompass perilously deep canyons, forested plateaus, and broad slickrock mesas. Water is at a premium in this extreme climate, much of which can be considered unforgiving desert, and permits are required.

None of the front-country hikes requires a permit. Most can be accessed directly from Zion Canyon Scenic Drive; a couple are in the Kolob Canyons section of the park. You can buy detailed guides and maps to the trails of Zion National Park at the Zion Canyon Visitor Center bookstore.

Note that the Narrows has a false reputation as accessible only via a two-day backcountry hike. On a dry, clear day, one look at the Virgin River at the end of Riverside Walk will demonstrate what many people figure out quite easily on their own: anyone can wade into the river upstream toward the Narrows; even better, no permit is required to travel the first 5 miles. Good hiking or wading boots are a must, and a walking stick is optional. You won't get far barefoot, and the slippery rocks can be too much for sandals. But you don't need to buy this gear; you can rent everything you need in Springdale. Past the first bend, you may spend as little as 50% of the time in the water (ranging from ankle-deep to waist-deep) as there are sandbars, small beaches, and short trails along the way. Be sure to ask a ranger about the potential for flash floods.

Whether you're heading out for a day of rock hopping or an hour of strolling, you should carry—and drink—plenty of water to counteract the effects of southern Utah's arid climate. Wear a hat, sunscreen, and sturdy shoes or boots; make sure to bring a map, and be honest with yourself about your capabilities. Getting in over your head can have serious health consequences.

Horseback Riding

Grab your hat and boots and see Zion Canyon the way the pioneers did—on the back of a horse or mule. This is a sure way to make your trip to Zion National Park memorable. Only one outfitter is licensed to guide tours within park boundaries.

Canyon Trail Rides

HORSEBACK RIDING | FAMILY | Easygoing, one-hour and half-day guided rides are available (minimum age 7 and 10 years, respectively). These friendly folks have been around for years and are the only outfitter for trail rides inside the park. Reservations are recommended and can be made online. The maximum weight is 220 pounds, and the season runs from March through October. ⊠ *Across from Zion Lodge, Zion National Park* ☎ *435/679–8665* ⊕ *www.canyonrides.com* 🖼 *From $45.*

Rock Climbing

The climbing in southern Utah is considered world-class. Keep your eyes peeled on Zion's scenic road for gearladen climbers heading up intimidating vertical faces. Park officials recommend March through May and September through November as the best times to climb inside the park. No permit is required.

Zion Rock and Mountain Guides

CLIMBING/MOUNTAINEERING | FAMILY | This company takes visitors (including families with children as young as four years old) on climbing, canyoneering, cycling, and jeep routes all over southern Utah's backcountry. (No outfitter can lead groups into Zion's legendary Narrows, Subway, or Orderville Canyon routes, although they can provide advice and equipment.) Friendly owner Dean Woods has been one of the region's eminent authorities on climbing since the 1970s. Costs depend on trip duration and group size: half-day family-climbing excursions range from $125 to $160 per person. Rates for biking trips, which include bikes and equipment, are similar. An all-day guided jeep tour to the area's highest peaks is $275 per person for two or more people. ⊠ *1458 Zion Park Blvd., Springdale* ☎ *435/772–3303* ⊕ *www.zionrockguides.com.*

Swimming

Swimming is allowed in the Virgin River, but be careful of cold water, slippery rock bottoms, and the occasional flash flood when it rains. Swimming is not permitted in the Emerald Pools. The use of inner tubes is prohibited within park boundaries, but some companies offer trips on a Virgin River tributary just outside the park.

Winter Activities

Cross-country skiing and snowshoeing are best experienced in the park's higher elevations in winter, where snow stays on the ground longer. Inquire at the Zion Canyon Visitor Center for backcountry conditions.

Chapter 4

ZION
GATEWAYS

Updated by
Shelley Arenas

⊙ Sights   🍴 Restaurants   🛏 Hotels   🛍 Shopping   🍸 Nightlife

★★★★☆   ★★★★☆   ★★★★☆   ★★★★☆   ★★★★☆

WELCOME TO ZION GATEWAYS

TOP REASONS TO GO

★ **Traveling through history:** Imagine life during pioneer days as you explore the historic sights of St. George.

★ **Blissing out:** Treat yourself at a luxuriant spa or partake of sophisticated dining (or both)—perhaps with views of crimson canyons.

★ **Gallery hopping:** Both Springdale and St. George have galleries featuring photography, paintings, and crafts that reflect the region and its aesthetic.

★ **Seeing red on the greens:** Golf courses in Hurricane and St. George feature fantastic red-rock backdrops.

1 Springdale. On the southern border of Zion National Park and featuring stunning views, this charming town of about 650 permanent residents hosts many of the park's 4+ million annual visitors. There are plenty of wonderful places to stay and eat, as well as some great shops and galleries along the main drag.

2 Hurricane. Pronounced "HURaken," this community on the Virgin River has experienced enormous growth, probably owing to the boom in nearby St. George. The town has one of Utah's most scenic 18-hole golf courses and is a less-expensive, less-crowded base for exploring Zion.

3 St. George. Bustling St. George offers every imaginable service: a regional airport, resort hotels, restaurants, a state university, and cultural activities. Situated 40 miles from Zion's entrance, it's a viable base for exploring the region. The Mormon settlement turned retirement community turned Sunbelt hub is also minutes from legalized gambling in Mesquite, Nevada.

4 Mount Carmel Junction. On Route 9, 13 miles east of the park, Mount Carmel Junction offers some funky small-town lodgings and the studio of Maynard Dixon, one of the finest painters of the American West.

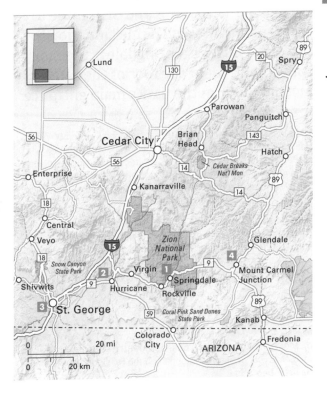

The region surrounding Zion National Park encompasses several small towns: Springdale, Hurricane, and St. George to the west and Mount Carmel Junction to the east. Of these, Springdale is the most convenient, set at the foot of the canyon just a mile from the park's main entrance.

Though inhabited by Native Americans as long ago as 500 AD, Springdale got its present-day name from Mormon farmers who settled here in 1862. About 50 years later, tourism in the region began to rise with the dawn of the automobile age and the 1909 establishment of the Mukuntuweap National Monument (which became Zion National Park in 1919).

The 1930 completion of the Zion–Mt. Carmel Highway and Tunnel made the area even easier to reach. Springdale kept apace, attracting travelers with a growing number of services and amenities. Today, the town continues the legacy of putting out the welcome mat—something it does very well.

With a population of more than 87,000, St. George, about 40 miles west of the park, is the region's biggest city, with several museums, good restaurants and hotels, and an airport that serves a few southwestern cities. The community, which was also settled by Mormons in the early 1860s, became the county seat in 1863, the same year construction began on the St. George Latter-day Saints Tabernacle.

This was followed by the St. George LDS Temple. Started in 1871 and dedicated in 1877, it was the first temple established west of the Mississippi River. Both it and the historic Winter Home of Brigham Young are open for tours. Other noteworthy attractions here include the Red Hills Desert Garden and Red Cliffs Desert Reserve.

The town of Hurricane is a suburb of St. George and close to the popular Gooseberry Mesa mountain-biking area. The unincorporated village of Mount Carmel Junction is best known for its Maynard Dixon Living History Museum and Gallery.

Planning

Hotels

Springdale has everything from small motels to quaint B&Bs to upscale hotels with modern amenities and riverside rooms. The booming community of St. George has scores of choices for any budget. Mount Carmel Junction has some funky, small-town options. To save the most money, however, consider staying in Hurricane.

Restaurants

Almost every restaurant in the region is family-friendly and hiker-casual. Springdale and St. George offer the most variety, from cafés that serve breakfast all day to lively bistros where you can dine outside and enjoy spectacular views. Note that some establishments don't serve alcohol and are closed on Sunday. A few also close seasonally.

Hotel and restaurant reviews have been shortened. For full information, visit Fodors.com. Restaurant prices are the average cost of a main course at dinner, or if dinner is not served, at lunch. Hotel prices are the lowest cost of a standard double room in high season.

What It Costs			
$	$$	$$$	$$$$
RESTAURANTS			
under $16	$16–$22	$23–$30	over $30
HOTELS			
under $125	$125–$175	$176–$225	over $225

Springdale

1.5 miles south of Zion National Park Visitor Center.

Although small, this gorgeously situated town of about 650 has more than doubled in population since 1990, thanks in large part to its being directly adjacent to Zion National Park. Hotels,

A collection of tombstones makes a fine epitaph for the ghost town of Grafton.

restaurants, and shops continue to pop up, yet Springdale still manages to maintain its small-town charm.

GETTING HERE AND AROUND

You'll need a car to get to Springdale, via Highway 9, but getting around once you're here is easy. The complimentary canyon-road shuttle bus—from February through November—makes getting from one end of Springdale to the other stress-free, with bus stops throughout town and connecting service to the free shuttle into Zion National Park. It's also a pleasant town to stroll through, with shops, galleries, and restaurants all in a central district. In winter, when there are fewer crowds, a car is handy for getting around town or visiting the park.

 Sights

Grafton

GHOST TOWN | FAMILY | A stone school, dusty cemetery, and a few wooden structures are all that remain of the nearby town of Grafton, which is between Springdale and Hurricane, a few miles west of the turnoff onto Bridge Road in Rockville. This ghost town has been featured in films such as *Butch Cassidy and the Sundance Kid.* ⊠ Hwy. 250 S.

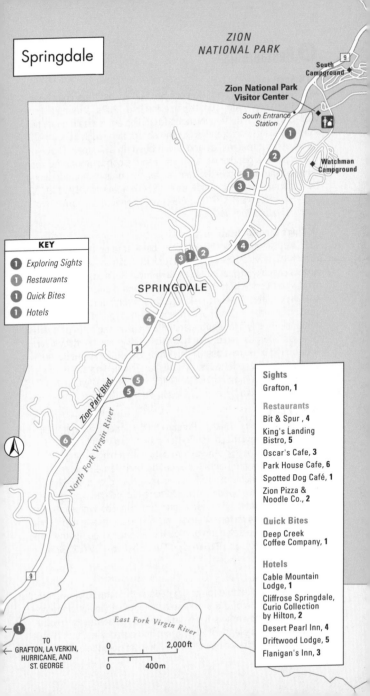

Springdale

ZION NATIONAL PARK

South Campground

Zion National Park Visitor Center

South Entrance Station

Watchman Campground

KEY

- ① *Exploring Sights*
- ① *Restaurants*
- ① *Quick Bites*
- ① *Hotels*

SPRINGDALE

Zion Park Blvd.

North Fork Virgin River

East Fork Virgin River

TO
←GRAFTON, LA VERKIN,
←HURRICANE, AND
ST. GEORGE

| 0 | 2,000ft |
| 0 | 400m |

Sights
Grafton, **1**

Restaurants
Bit & Spur , **4**
King's Landing
Bistro, **5**
Oscar's Cafe, **3**
Park House Cafe, **6**
Spotted Dog Café, **1**
Zion Pizza &
Noodle Co., **2**

Quick Bites
Deep Creek
Coffee Company, **1**

Hotels
Cable Mountain
Lodge, **1**
Cliffrose Springdale,
Curio Collection
by Hilton, **2**
Desert Pearl Inn, **4**
Driftwood Lodge, **5**
Flanigan's Inn, **3**

🍴 Restaurants

Bit & Spur

$$ | SOUTHWESTERN | This laid-back Springdale institution has been delighting locals and tourists since the late 1980s, offering a well-rounded menu that includes fresh fish and pasta dishes, but the emphasis is on creative Southwestern fare, such as roasted-sweet-potato tamales and chili-rubbed rib-eye steak. Craft beers and the popular house-made sangria complement the zesty cuisine. **Known for:** creative margaritas; live music; outdoor dining by a fountain beneath shade trees. $ *Average main: $20 ⌗ 1212 Zion Park Blvd.* ☎ *435/772–3498* ⊕ *www.bitandspur.com* ⊗ *No lunch. Closed Dec. and Jan.*

★ King's Landing Bistro

$$$ | MODERN AMERICAN | Request to be seated on the patio—with dramatic views of the area's red rock monoliths—when dining at this casually stylish bistro at downtown Springdale's popular Driftwood Lodge hotel. The artfully presented cuisine here tends toward creative American—king salmon with saffron couscous, roast chicken with artichoke tapenade—but you'll find some international, mostly Mediterranean, influences in the form of charred Spanish octopus and one or two outstanding pastas. **Known for:** interesting artisanal cocktail list; emphasis on local and seasonal produce and vegetables; rich desserts, including a classic tiramisu. $ *Average main: $24 ⌗ 1515 Zion Park Blvd.* ☎ *435/772–7422* ⊕ *www.klbzion.com* ⊗ *Closed Sun. No lunch.*

Oscar's Café

$ | SOUTHWESTERN | FAMILY | Prepare for an active day with a filling breakfast, or reward yourself after a long hike with lunch or dinner at this welcoming Southwestern café with a big, inviting patio offering stunning mountain views. The pork verde breakfast burrito and huevos rancheros are hearty and delicious, and excellent lunch and dinner options include flame-broiled garlic burgers topped with provolone cheese and shrimp tacos with a creamy lime sauce. **Known for:** blue-corn nachos with cheese and guacamole; extensive selection of creative burgers; large heated patio. $ *Average main: $15 ⌗ 948 Zion Park Blvd.* ☎ *435/772–3232* ⊕ *www.oscarscafe.com.*

Park House Cafe

$ | AMERICAN | Notable for its big patio with fantastic views into the park and for one of the better selections of vegan and vegetarian dishes in town, this funky little café decorated with colorful artwork serves plenty of tasty meat and egg dishes, too. The grilled ham Benedict has plenty of fans, as do buffalo burgers with havarti cheese and apple-pear-berry salads with organic greens, feta, and walnuts. **Known for:** breakfast served all day; full slate of espresso drinks and smoothies; ice cream sundaes and banana splits. ⑤ *Average main: $12* ⊠ *1880 Zion Park Blvd.* ☎ *435/772–0100* ⊘ *Closed Tues. No dinner.*

Spotted Dog Café

$$ | MODERN AMERICAN | At this upscale, light-filled restaurant with an eclectic menu that typically includes pastas and meat dishes, the staff makes you feel right at home even if you saunter in wearing hiking shoes. The exposed wood beams and large windows that frame the surrounding trees and rock cliffs set a Western mood, with tablecloths and original artworks supplying a dash of refinement. **Known for:** impressive but accessible wine list; lovely patio for alfresco dining; much of the produce is grown on site. ⑤ *Average main: $22* ⊠ *Flanigan's Inn, 428 Zion Park Blvd.* ☎ *435/772–0700* ⊕ *www.flanigans.com/dining* ⊘ *No lunch; no breakfast Oct.–May.*

Zion Pizza & Noodle Co.

$$ | PIZZA | FAMILY | Creative pizzas and a kickback atmosphere make this a great place to replenish after a trek through the canyon. Meat lovers can dive into the Cholesterol Hiker pizza, topped with pepperoni, Canadian bacon, and Italian sausage, but the Thai chicken and rosemary-garlic pies are also delicious. **Known for:** stone-slate pizzas with creative toppings; lovely garden seating; good craft beer list. ⑤ *Average main: $16* ⊠ *868 Zion Park Blvd.* ☎ *435/772–3815* ⊕ *www.zionpizzanoodle.com* ⊘ *No lunch. Closed Dec.–Feb.*

☕ Coffee and Quick Bites

★ Deep Creek Coffee Company

$ | CAFÉ | Stop by this cheerful coffeehouse with hanging plants and several tables on a spacious side patio to fuel up before your big park adventure or to grab some healthy sustenance for later. Hearty açaí and miso-quinoa bowls, avocado toast with poached eggs, bagels with the requisite schmears, breakfast burritos, and house-made granola are among the tasty offerings. **Known for:** opens at 6 am daily; refreshing house-made cold brew; delicious smoothies. ⑤ *Average main: $10* ⊠ *932 Zion Park Blvd.* ☎ *435/669–8849* ⊕ *www.deepcreekcoffee.com* ⊘ *No dinner.*

Hotels

★ Cable Mountain Lodge

$$$ | HOTEL | This contemporary lodge with a large swimming pool is the closest hotel in Springdale to Zion—it's a scenic five-minute walk over a footbridge across the Virgin River. **Pros:** steps from Zion National Park's south entrance; many suites have full kitchens; beautiful picnic area along river with gas grills and tables. **Cons:** no breakfast (but a coffeehouse and market steps away); not all rooms have park views; no pets. $ *Rooms from: $189* ⊠ *147 Zion Park Blvd.* ☎ *435/772–3366, 877/712–3366* ⊕ *www. cablemountainlodge.com* ⇆ *52 rooms* ⦿ *No meals.*

Cliffrose Springdale, Curio Collection by Hilton

$$$$ | HOTEL | The canyon views, acres of lush lawns and flowers, and pool and two-tier waterfall hot tubs at this stylish riverside hotel make it more than a place to rest your head, and you could throw a rock across the river and hit Zion National Park. **Pros:** close to Zion's south entrance; enchanting grounds and views; good restaurant serving breakfast and dinner. **Cons:** steep rates; lots of foot and car traffic nearby; no elevator. $ *Rooms from: $336* ⊠ *281 Zion Park Blvd.* ☎ *435/772–3234* ⊕ *www.cliffroselodge.com* ⇆ *52 rooms* ⦿ *No meals.*

★ Desert Pearl Inn

$$$$ | HOTEL | Offering spacious rooms with vaulted ceilings, oversize windows, sitting areas, small kitchens with wet bars and dishwashers, and a pleasing contemporary decor, this riverside lodge is special. **Pros:** spacious, smartly designed rooms; walking distance to restaurants; rooms facing river have balconies or terraces. **Cons:** often books up well in advance spring through fall; breakfast not included; pets not permitted. $ *Rooms from: $289* ⊠ *707 Zion Park Blvd.* ☎ *435/772–8888, 888/828–0898* ⊕ *www. desertpearl.com* ⇆ *73 rooms* ⦿ *No meals.*

Driftwood Lodge

$$$ | HOTEL | The rooms at this friendly roadside lodge are among the most reasonably priced in town, even for the premium units, which have balconies or patios along with great views of the Virgin River and surrounding canyons. **Pros:** excellent value; superb restaurant; attractive pool and picnic area. **Cons:** least expensive rooms have no view or balcony; breakfast not included; limited pet reservations must be booked by phone. $ *Rooms from: $189* ⊠ *1515 Zion Park Blvd., Springville* ☎ *435/772–3262* ⊕ *www. driftwoodlodge.net* ⇆ *63 rooms* ⦿ *No meals.*

Flanigan's Inn

$$ | HOTEL | A tranquil, nicely landscaped inn with canyon views and a small pool, Flanigan's has big, comfortable accommodations, including two private villas and suites that sleep six; some units have a patio or a deck. **Pros:** easy shuttle ride or pleasant walk to Zion Canyon Visitor Center; a meditation maze on the hilltop; great seasonal on-site café. **Cons:** not all rooms have views; smaller property that tends to book up quickly; breakfast, though discounted, isn't complimentary (and is unavailable in winter). $ *Rooms from: $159* ⊠ *450 Zion Park Blvd.* ☎ *435/772–3244* ⊕ *www.flanigans.com* 🛏 *34 rooms* ⦿ *No meals.*

 ## Nightlife

Zion Canyon Brew Pub

BREWPUBS/BEER GARDENS | Relax after a rugged day of hiking with a flight of ales in the beer garden of southern Utah's oldest craft beer maker, Zion Brewery, which is just steps from the park's southern entrance. The kitchen turns out decent pub grub, and there's live music most weekend evenings. ⊠ *95 Zion Park Blvd.* ☎ *435/772–0336* ⊕ *www.zionbrewery.com.*

 ## Shopping

David J. West Gallery

ART GALLERIES | The radiant photography of artist David West captures Zion's natural setting in its full grandeur, along with Bryce, Cedar Breaks, Arches, and other stunning spots throughout Utah and the Southwest. The gallery also stocks contemporary landscape paintings by Michelle Condrat and geologically inspired pottery by Bill Campbell. ⊠ *801 Zion Park Blvd.* ☎ *435/772–3510* ⊕ *www.davidjwest.com.*

Sol Foods Supermarket

FOOD/CANDY | Stop by this market specializing in healthy, organic foods for sandwiches, salads, and vegetarian snacks or box lunches for your adventures into the park. Also be sure to poke around the affiliated and well-stocked hardware and camping store next door. A few blocks closer to the park entrance, the owners also operate Hoodoos General Store, which dispenses espresso drinks, ice cream, pizza, and more gourmet goodies. ⊠ *995 Zion Park Blvd.* ☎ *435/772–3100* ⊕ *www.solfoods.com.*

★ Worthington Gallery

ART GALLERIES | The emphasis at this superb gallery set inside an 1880s pioneer home is on regional art, including pottery, works in glass, jewelry, beguiling copper wind sculptures by Lyman

In-the-know mountain bikers head to Gooseberry Mesa near the town of Hurricane.

Whitaker, and paintings that capture the dramatic beauty of southern Utah. ✉ *789 Zion Park Blvd.* ☎ *435/772–3446* ⊕ *www. worthingtongallery.com.*

Hurricane

22 miles west of Springdale; 18 miles northeast of St. George.

Only a half-hour from Zion, an increasing number of lodging establishments make Hurricane a fine alternate base for exploring "Dixie," a term referring to the area of south-central Washington County. Nearby Gooseberry Mesa is one of the best places for mountain biking in Utah.

GETTING HERE AND AROUND
From St. George, take I–5 north and then Highway 9 east. A car is a must in this area.

🍴 Restaurants

Main Street Café
$$ | **AMERICAN** | This colorful storefront eatery in historic downtown Hurricane pours one of the region's best cups of coffee, a fine prelude or follow-up to the salads, sandwiches, hearty omelets, homemade soups, flavorful pastas, and generous hamburgers on the menu. If you have the time, linger outside on the shaded patio and watch the hummingbirds. **Known for:** handy location for trips

east toward Zion National Park; pretty outdoor seating area; big portions. $ *Average main: $16* ⊠ *138 S. Main St.* ☎ *435/635–9080* ⊕ *www.mainstreetcafehurricane.com* ⊘ *Closed Sun.*

Hotels

Quality Inn Zion

$ | HOTEL | Though its rates can fluctuate, this is generally a more budget-friendly option than its counterparts just outside Zion, yet it's still within easy driving distance of the park. **Pros:** indoor room access; about 25 miles to Zion National Park; coin laundry on the premises. **Cons:** basic rooms; no restaurant; no elevator. $ *Rooms from: $100* ⊠ *43 N. 2600 W* ☎ *435/635–3500, 877/424–6423* ⊕ *www.choicehotels.com/utah/hurricane/quality-inn-hotels/ut420* 🛏 *53 rooms* ⦿ *Free Breakfast.*

🏃 Activities

Gooseberry Mesa

BICYCLING | The 13 miles of mountain-biking trails on this mesa near Hurricane, and about 40 miles east of St. George, are not well traveled, which is good news and bad news. On the plus side, there aren't hordes of fat-tire fanatics to spoil your view of the pristine desert wilderness. However, the trail itself, through gulches and canyons and across slickrock, can be hard to follow. At most major challenges along the path, there are easier alternatives if you lose your nerve. Come here for solitary and technical single-track challenges. ⊠ *Hurricane* ✢ *off Hwy. 59* ⊕ *www.blm. gov/visit/gooseberry-mesa-national-recreation-trail.*

Sky Mountain Golf Course

GOLF | Hurricane's public golf course, about 15 miles east of St. George, offers scenic views and among the most reasonable greens fees in the area. Many fairways are framed by red-rock outcroppings, and the course has a front-tee view of the nearby 10,000-foot Pine Valley Mountains. Don't get too distracted by the scenery—the back nine will require your full concentration. ⊠ *1030 N. 2600 W* ☎ *435/635–7888* ⊕ *www.skymountaingolf.com* 🏌 *$37–$57* 🏌 *18 holes, 6383 yards, par 72.*

St. George

18 miles southwest of Hurricane.

Believing the mild year-round climate ideal for growing cotton, Brigham Young dispatched 309 LDS families in 1861 to found

St. George. They were to raise cotton and silkworms and to establish a textile industry, to make up for textile shortages resulting from the Civil War.

The fifth fastest-growing metropolitan area in the country, St. George has become the cultural and recreational hub of southern Utah, a favorite place to relocate among both retirees who appreciate the warm winters and younger families and entrepreneurs lured by the high quality of life, stunning scenery, and growing number of restaurants, shops, and other services.

GETTING HERE AND AROUND

This burgeoning and increasingly sprawling city is bisected by Interstate 15, and although the very heart of downtown is pedestrian-friendly, you need a car to visit outlying attractions.

ESSENTIALS

Greater Zion Convention & Tourism Office

⊠ 20 N. Main St. ☎ 435/634–5747 ⊕ www.greaterzion.com.

Sights

Brigham Young Winter Home

HISTORIC SITE | Mormon leader Brigham Young spent the last seven winters of his life in the warm, sunny climate of St. George. Built of adobe on a sandstone-and-basalt foundation and now a museum, this two-story home, with pretty green and red trim and well-tended gardens, contains a portrait of Young over one fireplace and furnishings from the late 19th century. Visits are by guided tour. ⊠ 67 W. 200 N ☎ 435/673–2517 ⊕ history.churchofjesuschrist.org/landing/historic-sites ⊠ Free.

Kayenta Art Village

ARTS VENUE | In the heart of an upscale, contemporary planned community in Ivins, not far from Tuacahn Center for the Arts and Red Mountain Resort, this scenic little arts district contains several of southern Utah's top galleries, including Gallery 873, known for jewelry and ceramics; Kayenta Desert Arboretum & Desert Rose Labyrinth, which visitors can freely stroll through; Zia Pottery Studio, a co-op operated by talented local potters; and several others. Set against a red-rock landscape, it's an enchanting neighborhood to stroll through, especially during the Art in Kayenta outdoor festival in mid-October. Also check to see what's on at the Center for the Arts at Kayenta—which presents lectures, movies, theater, and concerts—or grab a bite at the excellent Xetava Gardens Cafe. ⊠ 875 Coyote Gulch Ct., Ivins ☎ 435/688–8535 ⊕ www.kayentautah.com.

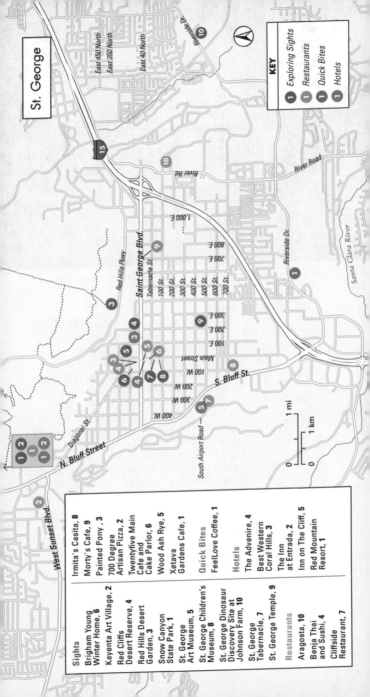

St. George

KEY
- **1** Exploring Sights
- **1** Restaurants
- **1** Quick Bites
- **1** Hotels

Sights

Brigham Young
Winter Home, **6**

Kayenta Art Village, **2**

Red Cliffs
Desert Reserve, **4**

Red Hills Desert
Garden, **3**

Snow Canyon
State Park, **1**

St. George
Art Museum, **5**

St. George Children's
Museum, **8**

St. George Dinosaur
Discovery Site at
Johnson Farm, **10**

St. George Tabernacle, **7**

St. George Temple, **9**

Restaurants

Aragosta, **10**

Benja Thai
and Sushi, **4**

Cliffside
Restaurant, **7**

Irmita's Casita, **8**

Morty's Cafe, **9**

Painted Pony, **3**

700 Degree
Artisan Pizza, **2**

Twentyfive Main
Cafe and
Cake Parlor, **6**

Wood Ash Rye, **5**

Xetava
Gardens Cafe, **1**

Quick Bites

FeelLove Coffee, **1**

Hotels

The Advenire, **4**

Best Western
Coral Hills, **3**

The Inn
at Entrada, **2**

Inn on The Cliff, **5**

Red Mountain
Resort, **1**

Mormon leader Brigham Young's former winter home is now a charming museum.

★ Red Cliffs Desert Reserve

NATURE PRESERVE | Encompassing the convergence of the Mojave, Great Basin, and Colorado Plateau desert zones, this pristine 62,000-acre tract of red-rock wilderness begins several miles north of St. George and was established in 2009 to protect the habitat of the desert tortoise. However, countless other flora and fauna—including gila monsters and chuckwallas—thrive in this unique transition zone that can be accessed through miles of designated hiking, mountain-biking, and horseback-riding trails. The best way to start your adventure is by visiting the reserve's contemporary visitor center (open weekdays only) in downtown St. George, where you'll find live animals, interactive exhibits, and staff who can advise you on hikes and other ways to visit. You can pick up trail maps here or download detailed PDF maps from the reserve website. The trail sections closest to St. George include City Creek and Paradise Canyon. Although it adjoins the reserve and is part of the same ecosystem, popular Snow Canyon State Park is administered separately. ⊠ *Visitor Center, 10 N. 100 E* ☎ *435/634–5759* ⊕ *www.redcliffsdesertreserve.com.*

★ Red Hills Desert Garden

GARDEN | Opened in 2015 as the state's first botanic garden devoted to desert conservation, Red Hills is a beautiful spot for a peaceful stroll as well as a great place to learn about water-efficient plants. More than 5,000 of them—including fragrant mesquite trees, prickly pear cactus, blue agave, Joshua trees, weeping yucca, and desert willows—thrive here, along with a meandering stream that's stocked with desert suckers, Virgin River chub, and other native species. Paths also lead past a number of boulders that preserve the tracks of dinosaurs that roamed here some 200 million years ago. The garden adjoins rugged Pioneer Park, a 52-acre expanse of rock-climbing and hiking terrain, with barbecue pits, picnic pavilions and tables, and both short and long trails. ⊠ *375 E. Red Hills Pkwy.* ☎ *435/673–3617* ⊕ *www.redhillsdesert-garden.com.*

★ Snow Canyon State Park
NATIONAL/STATE PARK | Named not for winter weather but after a pair of pioneering Utahans named Snow, this gem of a state park—about 10 miles north of St. George—is filled with natural wonders. Hiking trails lead to lava cones, sand dunes, cactus gardens, and high-contrast vistas. From the campground you can scramble up huge sandstone mounds and overlook the entire valley. Park staff lead occasional guided hikes. ⊠ *1002 Snow Canyon Dr., Ivins* ☎ *435/628–2255* ⊕ *stateparks.utah.gov/parks/snow-canyon* ⊠ *$15 per vehicle for nonresidents, $10 for Utah residents.*

St. George Art Museum
MUSEUM | **FAMILY** | The downtown centerpiece of St. George's growing art scene occupies an attractively reimagined former sugar-beet warehouse. The permanent collection celebrates the works of mostly regionally based potters, photographers, and painters, many of them depicting the region's spectacular landscapes. Rotating exhibits highlight local history and lore and showcase emerging contemporary talents. There's also a Family Discovery Center, with materials for kids to create their own works. ⊠ *47 E. 200 N* ☎ *435/627–4525* ⊕ *www.sgcity.org/artmuseum* ⊠ *$5* ⊗ *Closed Sun.*

St. George Children's Museum
MUSEUM | **FAMILY** | Located next to Town Square Park and the downtown library and set inside a former school building with a striking red-stone exterior, this impressive museum contains two floors of touch-friendly exhibits that will stimulate kids' imaginations, including an earthquake-simulation table, a science discovery lab, a transportation center with planes and an auto shop, and a miniature version of St. George's famed Tuacahn Amphitheatre. ⊠ *86 S. Main St.* ☎ *435/986–4000* ⊕ *www.sgchildrensmuseum. org* ⊠ *$5* ⊗ *Closed Mon.–Wed. except some Mon. holidays.*

St. George Dinosaur Discovery Site at Johnson Farm
ARCHAEOLOGICAL SITE | **FAMILY** | Unearthed in 2000 by property developers, this site preserves and exhibits ancient footprints left by dinosaurs from the Jurassic Period millions of years ago. Fossils unearthed here are also on display in the modern museum,

The St. George Temple (circa 1877) is southwest Utah's oldest Mormon house of worship.

where accurate replicas portray the creatures that left these tantalizing remains and themed displays cover many details of the Jurassic era. There's an interactive area for children and a Dino Park outside the museum with shaded picnic tables and a Walk Through Time exhibit. ⊠ *2180 E. Riverside Dr.* ☎ *435/574–3466* ⊕ *www.dinosite.org* ✉ *$8* 🕐 *Closed Tues. and Wed.*

St. George Tabernacle

HISTORIC SITE | This is one of the best-preserved pioneer buildings in the entire state, and it is still used for public meetings and programs for the community. Mormon settlers began work on the tabernacle just a few months after the city of St. George was established in June 1863. Upon completion of the sandstone building's 140-foot clock tower 13 years later, Brigham Young formally dedicated the site. You can visit the building by guided tour. ⊠ *18 S. Main St.* ☎ *435/229–8647* ⊕ *history.churchofjesuschrist. org/landing/historic-sites.*

St. George Temple

RELIGIOUS SITE | The red-sandstone temple, plastered over with white stucco, was completed in 1877 and was the first Mormon temple in southwest Utah. It has served as a meeting place for both Mormons and other congregations over the decades. Today, only members of the Church of Jesus Christ of Latter-day Saints can enter the temple, but a visitor center next door offers guided tours of the visitor center and grounds. ⊠ *250 E. 400 S* ☎ *435/673–5181* ⊕ *www.churchofjesuschrist.org/landing/ historic-sites.*

🍴 Restaurants

Aragosta

$$$$ | MODERN EUROPEAN | With a palatial dining room with chandeliers and white napery, this elegant restaurant east of downtown (and formerly in Ivins) specializes in haute American and European fare and is a favorite destination for special occasions. Think rich, creamy lobster bisque with Spanish sherry, risotto with black truffles and grilled prawns, fall-off-the-bone lamb osso buco, and chateaubriand for two. **Known for:** steaks with decadent sauces and sides; refined service; impressive wine list. ⑤ *Average main: $33* ✉ *1386 E. 100 S* ☎ *435/313–0611* ⊕ *www.aragostautah.com.*

Benja Thai and Sushi

$ | THAI | In a stone-walled dining room in downtown's charming Ancestor Square, you can dine on authentic hot-and-sour soups, papaya and larb salads, ginger chicken, whole crispy red snapper with spicy basil sauce, and other Thai dishes, as well as offerings from an extensive sushi menu. The room's tapestries, intricate wood carvings, and lilting music give it warmth and tranquility, and large windows provide views of the landscaped courtyard dotted with quaint historic buildings. **Known for:** huge selection of sushi rolls and nigiri; charming setting; mango cheesecake. ⑤ *Average main: $14* ✉ *2 W. St. George Blvd.* ☎ *435/628–9538* ⊕ *benjathai.com* ☾ *Closed Sun.*

Cliffside Restaurant

$$ | MODERN AMERICAN | This strikingly situated restaurant beside the Inn on the Cliff Hotel offers dazzling St. George Valley views from both the dining room and patio, making it an especially popular spot for sunset dinners. The kitchen turns out well-prepared modern American fare, with an emphasis on steaks and seafood—consider the seared flat-iron steak with chimichurri sauce or almond-crusted Idaho trout with farro pesto, broccolini, and a beurre blanc sauce. **Known for:** eye-popping views; buttermilk chicken-fried chicken; decadent, seasonally changing desserts. ⑤ *Average main: $22* ✉ *511 S. Tech Ridge Dr.* ☎ *435/319–6005* ⊕ *www.cliffsiderestaurant.com* ☾ *Closed Sun.*

Irmita's Casita

$ | MEXICAN | FAMILY | A standby for tasty Mexican-American fare in various locations around town since 1993, this humble spot serves affordable, no-nonsense food that can be quite spicy if requested. Specialties include spicy pork tortas, massive burritos smothered in red or green sauce, and shrimp enchiladas. **Known for:** steak chilaquiles at breakfast; chicken mole poblano; Mexican soft drinks and juices. ⑤ *Average main: $12* ✉ *95 W. 700 S*

☎ *435/703–9162* ⊕ *www.irmitascasita.net* ▤ *No credit cards* ⊘ *Closed Sun.*

Morty's Cafe

$ | MODERN AMERICAN | FAMILY | At this funky, updated take on a burger joint on the east side of downtown, the brick walls are hung with local art for sale. Creatively topped beef and veggie burgers are offered, plus breakfast burritos, several varieties of quinoa salad, and thick milkshakes. **Known for:** breakfast sandwiches and burritos served all day; three-bean veggie burgers with chipotle mayo; salted peanut-butter milkshakes. ⑤ *Average main: $8* ⊠ *702 E. St. George Blvd.* ☎ *435/359–4439* ⊕ *www.mortyscafe.com* ⊘ *Closed Sun.*

★ Painted Pony

$$$$ | MODERN AMERICAN | Shaded patio dining overlooking Ancestor Square and contemporary Southwestern art on the walls provides a romantic setting for enjoying contemporary American fare with an emphasis on seasonal ingredients, many from the owners' private organic garden. Consider sage-smoked quail with a tamarind glaze, followed by a juniper-brined bone-in pork chop with stuffed pears and smoked-tomato relish, and don't pass up the standout sides that include sweet cornbread pudding, truffle potato chips, and Stilton fritters. **Known for:** knowledgeable servers; one of the best wine lists in town; seasonally changing bread pudding. ⑤ *Average main: $32* ⊠ *2 W. St. George Blvd.* ☎ *435/634–1700* ⊕ *www.painted-pony.com* ⊘ *No lunch Sun.*

700 Degree Artisan Pizza

$ | PIZZA | After a hike in nearby Pioneer Park or Red Hills Desert Garden, fuel up on delicious blistered-crust pizzas at this hip eatery and taproom that's also known for its impressive selection of craft beers and sodas as well as wines on tap. Favorite pies include the Arugula Bianca with roasted garlic, prosciutto, pecorino Romano, and truffle oil and the spice-lover's Purgatory, which has a spicy tomato base along with Calabrese salami, pepperoncini, jalapeños, and sweet-and-hot Italian sausage. **Known for:** pizzas with interesting toppings; wood-fired meatballs, garlic bread, and other sides; dessert pizzas topped with Nutella and ricotta cheese. ⑤ *Average main: $14* ⊠ *974 W. Sunset Blvd.* ☎ *435/703–6700* ⊕ *www.700degree.pizza* ⊘ *Closed Mon.*

TwentyFive Main Cafe and Cupcake Parlor

$ | CAFÉ | With bird's-egg-blue cuckoo clocks and light-hearted Victorian-theme prints on the walls, this café in St. George's historic downtown is all about whimsy and fun, right down to the to-die-for homemade cupcakes, such as orange blossom and chocolate espresso. Lunch offerings include pastas, panini, deli sandwiches, and salads. **Known for:** cupcakes galore; hip vibe; live music. ⑤ *Average main: $10* ⊠ *25 N. Main St.* ☎ *435/628–7110* ⊕ *25main. com* ⊗ *Closed Sun.*

★ Wood Ash Rye

$$$ | MODERN AMERICAN | With a white-tile open kitchen, marble tables, and a wood-beam ceiling, this scene-y farm-to-table restaurant and bar in the swanky Advenire Hotel has quickly become St. George's destination for people-watching and deftly crafted seasonal cuisine. The sharing-friendly menu changes regularly but always features a selection of cheeses and charcuterie, and typical offerings include grilled octopus with preserved lemon and smoked olive oil, pan-seared scallops with risotto in Mornay sauce, and duck tacos. **Known for:** innovative cocktails and mocktails; oysters served raw, charbroiled, or fried; rotating selection of house-made ice creams and sorbets. ⑤ *Average main: $25* ⊠ *25 W. St. George Blvd.* ☎ *435/522–5020* ⊕ *www.theadvenirehotel. com.*

★ Xetava Gardens Cafe

$$ | MODERN AMERICAN | This beautifully designed adobe oasis in the Kayenta Art Village in Ivins, about 10 miles northwest of St. George, offers gracious indoor and outdoor seating, the latter overlooking fragrant high-desert gardens. Pronounced Zah-Tah-Vah, the space began as a coffee bar and is still a source of lattes and mochas, but you'll also find an eclectic selection of globally inspired all-day fare, including ham ciabattas, wild-caught mahimahi green curry, peach-glazed organic chicken, and wild mushroom burgers. **Known for:** location near several art galleries; well-curated beer, wine, and cocktail list; croissant bread pudding with caramel sauce. ⑤ *Average main: $17* ⊠ *815 Coyote Gulch Ct., Ivins* ☎ *435/656–0165* ⊕ *www.xetava.com* ⊗ *No dinner Mon.–Wed.*

☕ Coffee and Quick Bites

FeelLove Coffee

$ | CAFÉ | Head to this light-filled, high-ceilinged café just off the east side's Virgin River bike and jogging trail for well-crafted coffees, teas, and lemonades as well as an assortment of tasty, generally healthy, dishes. Start the day with an egg-avocado toast or a turmeric-tofu scramble, and for lunch, try the vegan Greek salad, turkey–Munster cheese baguette, or "nachos" topped with sliced apples, date caramel, almond butter, and pistachios. **Known for:** lots of vegan options; Thai, matcha, and other sweet tea lattes; fresh-baked desserts, including many vegan options. ⑤ *Average main: $10* ⊠ *558 E. Riverside Dr.* ☎ *435/922–1717* ⊕ *www.feello-vecoffee.com.*

Hotels

The Advenire

$$$ | HOTEL | A strikingly contemporary, upscale hotel that's directly across the street from the buzzy shopping and dining of Ancestor Square, this stylish member of Marriott Bonvoy's indie-spirited Autograph Collection exudes hipness with its hardwood floors, bold-print pillows and chairs, high-tech entertainment centers, and cushy bedding. **Pros:** stylish, cosmopolitan decor; superb on-site restaurant; steps from downtown dining and retail. **Cons:** neighborhood can be crowded and noisy at times; steep cleaning fee if you bring a pet; parking is pricey and valet only unless you find a spot on the street. ⑤ *Rooms from: $184* ✉ *25 W. St. George Blvd.* ☎ *435/522–5022* ⊕ *www.theadvenirehotel.com* ⇨ *60 rooms* ⑩ *No meals.*

Best Western Coral Hills

$ | HOTEL | FAMILY | This reasonably priced two-story motel set against a backdrop of red hills is a handy choice for being a short walk from many restaurants, shops, and downtown attractions, and heated indoor and outdoor pools promise relaxation after a busy day. **Pros:** suites have deep jetted tubs; pool and hot tub set within a red rock grotto; lots of dining options nearby. **Cons:** some issues with street noise; breakfast is basic; kids often congregate around the pools. ⑤ *Rooms from: $108* ✉ *125 E. St. George Blvd.* ☎ *435/673–4844* ⊕ *www.coralhills.com* ⇨ *98 rooms* ⑩ *Free breakfast.*

The Inn at Entrada

$$$ | HOTEL | Hikers, spa goers, and—above all—golfers flock to this plush boutique resort set amid the red-rock canyons northwest of downtown, surrounded by a world-class Johnny Miller–designed golf course, and offering a top-notch spa, pool, and fitness facility. **Pros:** adjoins one of the top golf courses in the state; attractive Southwest-inspired contemporary decor; terrific spa. **Cons:** 10- to 15-minute drive from downtown dining; some guests have noted noise from thin walls and construction; can get very expensive depending on time of year. ⑤ *Rooms from: $199* ✉ *2588 W. Singua Trail* ☎ *435/634–7100* ⊕ *www.innatentrada.com* ⇨ *57 rooms* ⑩ *No meals.*

★ Inn on the Cliff

$$$ | HOTEL | It's all about the panoramic views at this exceptionally well-maintained midcentury modern boutique hotel set high on a ridge overlooking downtown St. George and the red rocks beyond. **Pros:** reasonable rates for such a nice property; stunning views; continental breakfast delivered to your room. **Cons:** breakfast is a bit meager; too far to walk from downtown; restaurant closed on Sunday. Ⓢ *Rooms from: $179* ✉ *511 S. Tech Ridge Dr.* ☎ *435/216–5864* ⊕ *www.innonthecliff.com* ⇥ *27 rooms* ⦿ *Free breakfast.*

★ Red Mountain Resort

$$$$ | RESORT | This luxurious red-rock hideaway, with its stunning surroundings near the mouth of Snow Canyon, offers a range of outdoor adventures and fitness and wellness options, from fitness classes, hikes, and yoga sessions to red clay–lavender body wraps and warm Himalayan salt stone massages. **Pros:** world-class spa and fitness facilities; handsome contemporary design fits in with natural surroundings; a range of meal, spa, and activity packages available. **Cons:** caters more to activity-seekers than those looking to relax; 15-minute drive northwest of St. George; all those potential treatment, activity, and meal add-ons can get pricey. Ⓢ *Rooms from: $235* ✉ *1275 E. Red Mountain Circle, Ivins* ☎ *435/673–4905, 877/246–4453* ⊕ *www.redmountainresort.com* ⇥ *106 units* ⦿ *No meals.*

Nightlife

★ George's Corner

BARS/PUBS | A lively hub of bustling Ancestor Square, this welcoming tavern is open all day for casual dining but is also one of the city's relatively few late-night options for drinks and live music. The spacious bar decorated with historic black-and-white photos of the area offers a nice selection of cocktails and regional craft brews. ✉ *2 W. St. George Blvd.* ☎ *435/216–7311* ⊕ *www.georgescornerrestaurant.com.*

Zion Brewery Station II Bar

BREWPUBS/BEER GARDENS | Southwestern Utah's best craft brewery is based in Springdale but also operates this hip taproom with pool tables and a patio near Ancestor Square. ✉ *142 N. Main St.* ☎ *435/673–7644* ⊕ *www.zionbrewery.com.*

 Performing Arts

Tuacahn

CONCERTS | At this magnificent outdoor amphitheater nestled in a natural red-sandstone cove, you can watch touring Broadway musicals and concerts by noted pop artists. ✉ *1100 Tuacahn Dr., Ivins* ☎ *800/746–9882 box office, 435/652–3300 administration* ⊕ *www.tuacahn.org.*

Petrified sand dunes are among the red-rock formations in Snow Canyon State Park.

Shopping

★ Rowley's Red Barn

FOOD/CANDY | FAMILY | Set in a red barn just a 10-minute drive northeast of St. George, this outpost of the legendary family farm and fruitstand in central Utah is a favorite stop for delicious apples, cherries, peaches, pears, and watermelons, along with several items grown out-of-state, including oranges and pineapples. Be sure to sample the fresh-pressed apple juice and cider. The ice cream parlor doles out tasty treats, including shakes and apple-cider slushes. ✉ *25 N. 300 W, Washington* ☎ *435/652–6611* ⊕ *www.rowleysredbarn.com* ⊙ *Closed Sun.*

Urban Renewal

HOUSEHOLD ITEMS/FURNITURE | In the heart of Ancestor Square's retail district, this big housewares emporium carries all sorts of fun curiosities and gifts for the home, from larger tables and chairs to antique farm implements, vintage toys and collectibles, old books, interesting kitchen goods, and more. ✉ *5 E. 100 N* ☎ *435/236–3838* ⊕ *www.facebook.com/byjennylarsen.*

Activities

BICYCLING

Bicycles Unlimited

BICYCLING | A trusted southern Utah biking resource, this shop rents bikes and sells parts and accessories and also offers

maps and advice about great rides in the area. ✉ *90 S. 100 E*
☎ *435/673–4492, 888/673–4492 ⊕ www.bicyclesunlimited.com.*

GOLF
★ Entrada at Snow Canyon Country Club
GOLF | Opened in 1996 and surrounded by a spectacular desert landscape, this challenging course designed by Johnny Miller is ranked among the top courses in the Southwest for its perfectly manicured greens and stylish clubhouse. This is a private course, but it is accessible to guests staying at the Inn at Entrada, which offers stay-and-play packages. ✉ *2511 W. Entrada Trail* ☎ *435/986–2200 ⊕ www.golfentrada.com* 🎫 *$110–$150* 🏌 *18 holes, 7062 yards, par 72.*

The Ledges Golf Course
GOLF | Seven miles north of St. George, this state-of-the-art course designed by Matt Dye features meticulously maintained greens and an impressive backdrop of red rock combined with panoramic views of Snow Canyon State Park. The difficult back nine may be a bit intimidating for less experienced golfers. ✉ *1585 Ledges Pkwy.* ☎ *435/634–4640 ⊕ www.ledges.com/golf-course* 🎫 *$75–$120* 🏌 *18 holes, 7200 yards, par 72.*

Mount Carmel Junction

13 miles east of Zion National Park east entrance via Rte. 9 east.

Little more than where Highway 9 meets U.S. 89, Mount Carmel Junction does offer some funky small-town lodging for those willing to stay about 15 minutes east of Zion National Park's east entrance. Don't miss the studio of Maynard Dixon, the artist many consider the finest painter of the American West.

GETTING HERE AND AROUND
From St. George, it's nearly 66 miles northeast via I–15 to Exit 16, then east on Highway 9.

 Sights

Maynard Dixon Living History Museum and Gallery
MUSEUM | Two miles north of Mount Carmel Junction, you can tour the final summer residence of the famous painter of Western life and landscapes. Dixon lived from 1875 to 1946 and was married to the renowned WPA photographer Dorothea Lange, and, following their divorce, to San Francisco muralist Edith Hamlin. He and Hamlin summered on this property from 1939 until his death; shortly after his death, she scattered his ashes on a ridge behind

the property, which consists of the original log cabin structure and an exceptional Western Art gallery, both of which are maintained by the nonprofit Thunderbird Foundation for the Arts. From March through November, self-guided and docent-led tours (by appointment only) are offered. The gallery and gift shop are open daily year-round. ⊠ *2200 S. State St. (U.S. 89), Mount Carmel* ☎ *435/648–2653* ⊕ *www.thunderbirdfoundation.com* ✉ *Gallery free, self-guided tours $10, guided tours $20.*

Hotels

Best Western East Zion Thunderbird Lodge

$$ | HOTEL | About 13 miles beyond the east entrance of Zion National Park, this low-slung motel with clean, spacious rooms decorated with rustic lodge-style furniture is a good option if you also want to be within an hour's drive of Bryce Canyon National Park. **Pros:** restaurant serves delicious pies; outdoor heated pool, hot tub; well-manicured grounds. **Cons:** no elevator; 20-minute drive to Kanab restaurants; breakfast not included. ⑤ *Rooms from: $159* ⊠ *4530 State St. (U.S. 89)* ☎ *435/648–2203 hotel direct, 800/780–7234 reservations* ⊕ *www.bestwestern.com* ➴ *61 rooms* ⑩*No meals.*

Zion Ponderosa Ranch Resort

$$$$ | RESORT | FAMILY | Just a few miles beyond Zion National Park's east entrance and about 16 miles northwest of Mount Carmel Junction, this scenic, 4,000-acre ranch offers a varied lineup of lodgings and a dizzying array of activities. **Pros:** lots of family-friendly activities; tranquil setting near Zion's east entrance; off-season packages include breakfast and Jeep tours. **Cons:** pool gets crowded in summer; very kid-centric; not many dining options nearby. ⑤ *Rooms from: $249* ⊠ *Twin Knolls Rd., Orderville* ☎ *435/648–2700, 800/293–5444* ⊕ *www.zionponderosa.com* ➴ *31 cabins* ⑩*No meals.*

BRYCE CANYON NATIONAL PARK

Updated by
Shelley Arenas

⛰ Camping   🛏 Hotels   🎿 Activities   👁 Scenery   👥 Crowds

★★★★★   ★★★★☆   ★★★★★   ★★★★★   ★★★☆☆

WELCOME TO BRYCE CANYON NATIONAL PARK

TOP REASONS TO GO

★ **Hoodoo heaven:** The boldly colored, gravity-defying limestone tentacles reaching skyward—called hoodoos—are Bryce Canyon's most recognizable attraction.

★ **Famous fresh air:** With some of the clearest skies in the nation, the park offers views that, on a clear day, can extend nearly 200 miles and into three states.

★ **Spectacular sunrises and sunsets:** The deep orange and crimson hues of the park's hoodoos are intensified by the light of the sun at either end of the day.

★ **Dramatically different zones:** From the highest point of the rim to the canyon base, the park spans 2,000 feet, so you can explore three unique climatic zones: spruce-fir forest, ponderosa-pine forest, and pinyon pine–juniper forest.

★ **Snowy fun:** Bryce gets an average of 87 inches of snowfall a year and is a popular destination for skiers and snowshoe enthusiasts.

1 Bryce Amphitheater. From this, the heart of the park, you can access the historic Bryce Canyon Lodge as well as Sunrise, Sunset, and Inspiration points. Walk to Bryce Point at sunrise to view the mesmerizing collection of massive hoodoos known as Silent City.

2 Under-the-Rim. The best way to reach the backcountry is along this 23-mile trail. It can be a challenging three-day adventure or half day of fun via one of four main-road access points. Primitive campgrounds dot the route.

3 Rainbow and Yovimpa Points. The end of the scenic road, but not of the scenery, here you can hike a trail to see ancient bristlecone pines and look south into Grand Staircase–Escalante National Monument.

4 Bryce Canyon City. Just a few miles from the visitor center on the shuttle route, this "company town" was incorporated in 2007 by the owners of Ruby's Inn nearly a century after it first welcomed guests. Though it has fewer than 200 year-round residents, thousands of annual visitors make it their base.

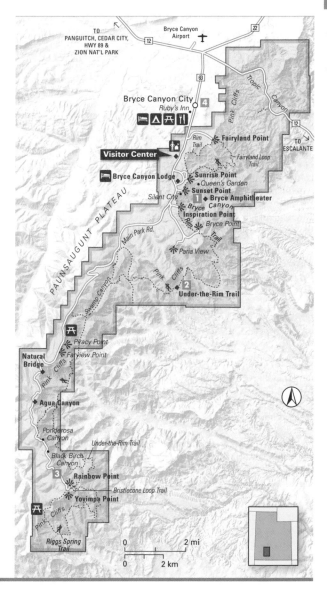

TO
PANGUITCH, CEDAR CITY,
HWY 89 &
ZION NAT'L PARK

Bryce Canyon
Airport

12

22

Bryce Canyon City   4
Ruby's Inn

Pink Cliffs

Tropic

Canyon

12

TO
ESCALANTE

Rim
Trail

Fairyland Point

Fairyland Loop
Trail

Visitor Center

Bryce Canyon Lodge

Sunrise Point
Queen's Garden
Sunset Point

Bryce Amphitheater   1

Silent City

Bryce   Canyon

Inspiration Point

Bryce Point

PAUNSAUGUNT   PLATEAU

Main Park Rd.

Rim

Trail

Paria View

Pink   Cliffs

Swamp Canyon

Under-the-Rim Trail   2

Piracy Point

Fairview Point

Natural
Bridge

Pink   Cliffs

Agua Canyon

Ponderosa
Canyon

Under-the-Rim Trail

Black Birch
Canyon

Rainbow Point   3

Bristlecone Loop Trail

Yovimpa Point

Pink   Cliffs

Riggs Spring
Trail

0   2 mi

0   2 km

A land that captures the imagination and the heart, Bryce is a favorite among the Southwest's national parks. Although its splendor has always rivaled that of Zion, Bryce Canyon wasn't designated a national park until a decade after its sibling was established.

The park is named for hard-luck pioneer rancher Ebenezer Bryce, who famously remarked that the Bryce Amphitheater is "a hell of a place to lose a cow." A Scottish immigrant sent to the area by the Mormon Church to begin an agricultural community, he created an irrigation ditch for his crops and built a road through the cliffs to make it easier to transport timber from the forests. The road ended at the amphitheater, and people started calling the area "Bryce's Canyon."

Due to the challenges of farming in the area, he departed the valley below the canyon (for Arizona) five years after arriving, as did other settlers. In the early 1900s, conservationists concerned about damage to the lands—from overuse by visitors and increased logging—lobbied for federal protection of the area. The government did so in 1923, first by designating it a national monument, and then, a year later, by establishing it as Utah National Park. It was given its current name in 1928.

Within Bryce's approximately 56 square miles (one-fourth the size of Zion) lie three distinct temperate zones; countless species of birds, animals, and flora; a scenic drive; more than a dozen trails; and tens of millions of years of geological history. Among the byproducts of this history are Bryce Canyon's fanciful rock formations known as hoodoos, which are particularly spectacular at sunrise or sunset when the light plays off the red rock. Bryce continues to evolve today, with old hoodoos crumbling (as erosion undercuts the soft rock beneath the harder, caprock top layer) and new ones forming as the amphitheater rim recedes.

The high plateau, with the visitor center, scenic drive, and Ruby's Inn, is named Paunsaugunt, the Paiute word for "home of the beaver." At an elevation of more than 8,000 feet, it's covered by hardy pines, inhabited by deer and small mammals, and surrounded by clean air. Its rim gives way to an otherworldly landscape that attracts more than a million visitors per year.

AVERAGE HIGH/LOW TEMPERATURES (FAHRENHEIT)					
JAN.	**FEB.**	**MAR.**	**APR.**	**MAY**	**JUNE**
37/15	38/17	45/23	54/29	64/37	75/45
JULY	**AUG.**	**SEPT.**	**OCT.**	**NOV.**	**DEC.**
80/53	77/50	70/42	58/32	45/23	36/15

Planning

When to Go

Around Bryce Canyon National Park and the nearby Cedar Breaks National Monument area, elevations approach and surpass 9,000 feet, making for temperamental weather, intermittent and seasonal road closures due to snow, and downright cold nights well into June. The air is cooler on the rim of the canyon than it is at lower altitudes. ■TIP→ **If you choose to see Bryce Canyon from April through October, you'll be visiting with the rest of the world. During this period, traffic on the main road can be heavy and parking limited, so consider taking one of the park shuttle buses. RV access is also limited to a handful of lots and camping areas, most of them near the park entrance, during these months.**

If it's solitude you're looking for, come to Bryce anytime between November and February. The park is open all year long, so if you come during the cooler months, you might just have a trail all to yourself.

Getting Here and Around

AIR

The nearest commercial airport to Bryce Canyon, Cedar City Regional Airport is 80 miles west and has daily direct flights from Salt Lake City. The airports in Salt Lake City and Las Vegas are the closest major ones to the park—each is about a four-hour drive.

BUS

A shuttle bus system operates in Bryce Canyon from mid-April through mid-October. Buses start at 8 am and run every 10 to 15 minutes until 8 pm in summer and 6 pm in early spring and October; they're free once you pay park admission. The route begins at the Shuttle Station north of the park, where parking is available (visitors can also park at Ruby's Inn or Ruby's Campground outside

Great Itineraries

BRYCE CANYON IN ONE DAY

Begin your day at the **visitor center** just past the park entrance. Pick up the current park guide and Junior Ranger booklets for the kids, and watch the 20-minute overview film. Sign up for a ranger-led hike or talk (for adults and/ or kids): it will be the most interesting and informative 60 minutes you spend in the park.

Presuming you have the better part of a day, beat the crowds by driving all the way to the park's south end for your first look at the canyon at **Rainbow Point**. From here, a short, rolling hike along the **Bristlecone Loop Trail** takes you through a forest of bristlecone pines and rewards you with spectacular views. On a clear day, you'll be able to see south to the Grand Canyon, east to Grand Staircase National Monument, and west across the Paunsaugunt Plateau.

Start working your way back to **Bryce Point**, allowing two to three hours for the drive and stops at select viewpoints, such as **Agua Canyon**, **Natural Bridge**, and **Farview Point**. This will enable you to save a half-day for the **Bryce Amphitheater** at the heart of the park. Begin your explorations at **Bryce Canyon Lodge** or **General Store** if you need to eat or replenish snacks.

Enjoy a relaxing hike along the **Rim Trail**, or drop down into the canyon on one of the park's signature short hikes. The easiest route is the **Queen's Garden Trail** at Sunrise Point. If you're a little more ambitious, take the steep switchbacks of the **Navajo Loop** to **Wall Street**. Remember that almost all Bryce hikes feature a sharp descent into the canyon at the outset, which unfortunately means a rigorous climb to exit. Most of the plateau is at or above 8,000 feet, so be aware of the thin air and risk of sunburn.

End your day with dinner at **Bryce Canyon Lodge** (you'll want to have made your reservations that morning). Try to time sunset to be at an overlook: **Inspiration Point**, **Sunset Point**, and **Bryce Point** each offer memorable vistas. As you leave the park, stop at **Ruby's Inn** for Native American jewelry, souvenirs, hand-dipped ice cream cones, or any other supplies for the road.

BRYCE CANYON IN THREE DAYS

Your choice of lodging will help you define three unforgettable days in Bryce. For the consummate historical experience, reserve (well in advance!) a cabin at **Bryce Canyon Lodge**. For starry-sky nights and a likely visit from mule deer, choose either campground in the park. For a few more amenities, stay at the sprawling **Ruby's Inn** or one of the other lodgings in Bryce Canyon City just outside the park.

As dawn breaks on your first day, consult with rangers at the **visitor center** and choose a ranger-led talk or hike that suits your interests and schedule. Then head into the canyon at **Sunrise Point**, combining the **Queen's Garden** and **Navajo trails**. You can see Queen Victoria, Thor's Hammer, and Wall Street, three of the park's most famous icons. Relax and recover from this moderate hike with the 18-mile scenic drive, stopping to see **Agua Canyon**, **Natural Bridge**, and **Bryce Point**. Wherever you are on the plateau, keep your eyes open for deer, prairie dogs, and dozens of bird species. Refuel from the day's adventures with pizza on the patio at **Valhalla Pizzeria**, next to the Bryce Canyon Lodge.

On Day 2, skip the crowds by descending into the canyon for a half-day hike. **Peekaboo Loop** (three to four hours) takes you to see the Wall of Windows; **Fairyland Loop** (four to five hours) takes you to Tower Bridge and China

Wall; **Agua Canyon** (four to five hours) gives you a taste of the famed Under-the-Rim Trail and a view of Natural Bridge from below. End your day with dinner at **Bryce Canyon Lodge** (you'll want to have made your reservations that morning). Try to time sunset to be at an overlook: **Inspiration Point**, **Sunset Point**, and **Bryce Point** offer memorable vistas.

On your final day, savor the perspectives from **Fairyland Point** or Bryce Point, then return to **Highway 12** (a national scenic byway). If you're headed west, spend an hour exploring **Red Canyon** (10 miles from the turnoff for Bryce) in Dixie National Forest; the 0.8-mile Bird's Eye Trail is a kid-friendly hike from the informative visitor center. Save room for a slice of homemade pie at Bryce Canyon Pines restaurant and motel. If you're headed east, hike to **Mossy Cave** (within Bryce Canyon National Park but accessible only from Highway 12), a short 1-mile round-trip that showcases Bryce's floral diversity and a small waterfall. Have dinner in Tropic at the Stone Hearth Grille, which has a deck with sweeping vistas.

the park entrance and catch the shuttle there). It stops at the visitor center, lodge, campgrounds, and all the main overlooks and trailheads.

CAR

The closest major cities to Bryce Canyon are Salt Lake City and Las Vegas, each about 270 miles away. You reach the park via Highway 63, just off of Highway 12, which connects U.S. 89 just south of Panguitch with Torrey, near Capitol Reef National Park. You can see the park's highlights by driving along the well-maintained road running the length of the main scenic area. Bryce has no restrictions on automobiles on the main road, but from spring through fall you may encounter heavy traffic and full parking lots—it's advisable to take the shuttle bus at this time.

Inspiration

Bryce Canyon Auto and Hiking Guide, by Tully Stroud, includes information on the geology and history of the area.

Shadows of Time: The Geology of Bryce Canyon National Park, by Frank Decourten with photographs by John Telford, explains regional geology and points out things to look for at park overlooks. An updated edition of this book was published in 2014 by Bryce Canyon Natural History Association, the park's nonprofit partner, which sells books and souvenirs at the visitor center and online at ⊕ *www.brycecanyon.org.*

Supplement the free park map with *National Geographic's Trails Illustrated's Bryce Canyon Map,* which includes a detailed park hiking map, trail descriptions, and photographs.

To prepare elementary-school kids for a trip to the park, consider ordering *Bryce Canyon,* by Jennifer Hackett, part of a series called "A True Book: National Parks" that depicts park history, geology, scenery, plants, and animals. Get the companion books on Zion and the Grand Canyon if your family plans to visit those parks, too.

The 2006 movie *Outlaw Trail: The Treasure of Butch Cassidy* was filmed at several locations in Utah, including Bryce Canyon. Available on DVD, it tells the story of the teen great-nephew of Butch Cassidy and how he defended the name of his outlaw uncle.

Park Essentials

ACCESSIBILITY

Most park facilities were constructed between 1930 and 1960. Some have been upgraded for wheelchair accessibility, while others can be used with some assistance. The Sunset Campground offers two sites with wheelchair access. Few of Bryce's trails, however, can be managed in a standard wheelchair due to the sandy, rocky, or uneven terrain. The section of the Rim Trail between Sunrise and Inspiration points is wheelchair accessible. The 1-mile Bristlecone Loop Trail at Rainbow Point has a hard surface and could be used with assistance, but several grades do not meet accessibility standards. Accessible parking is marked at all overlooks and public facilities.

PARK FEES

The entrance fee is $35 per vehicle for a seven-day pass and $20 for pedestrians or bicyclists, which includes unlimited use of the park shuttle. An annual Bryce Canyon park pass, good for one year from the date of purchase, costs $40. If you leave your private vehicle outside the park at the shuttle staging area or Ruby's Inn or Campground, the one-time entrance fee is $35 per party and includes transportation on the shuttle.

A $5 backcountry permit, available from the visitor center, is required for camping in the park's interior, allowed only on Under-the-Rim Trail and Rigg's Spring Loop, both south of Bryce Point. Campfires are not permitted.

PARK HOURS

The park is open 24/7, year-round. It's in the Mountain Time Zone.

CELL PHONE RECEPTION

Cell phone reception is hit-or-miss in the park, with some of the higher points along the main road your best bet. The lodge and visitor center have limited (it can be slow during busy periods) Wi-Fi, and there are pay phones at a few key spots in the park, but these are gradually being removed.

Hotels

Lodgings in and around Bryce Canyon include both rustic and modern options, but all fill up fast in summer. Bryce Canyon Lodge is the only hotel inside the park, but there are a number of options in Bryce Canyon City, just north of the park's entrance.

Nearby Panguitch and Tropic, and Escalante a bit farther away, are small towns with a number of additional budget and mid-range hotels, and these places tend to have more last-minute availability. Other gateway towns include Brian Head and Cedar City; both are more than an hour away so are best used as stops on a multiday road trip through the region.

Restaurants

Dining options in the park proper are limited to a few options in or near Bryce Canyon Lodge; you'll also find a handful of restaurants serving mostly standard American fare within a few miles of the park entrance, in Bryce Canyon City. Venture farther afield—to Tropic and Escalante to the east, and Panguitch and Hatch to the west—and the diversity of culinary offerings increases a bit.

Hotel and restaurant reviews have been shortened. For full information, visit Fodors.com. Restaurant prices are the average cost of a main course at dinner, or if dinner is not served, at lunch. Hotel prices are the average cost of a standard double room in high season, excluding taxes and service charges.

What It Costs			
$	$$	$$$	$$$$
RESTAURANTS			
under $16	$16–$22	$23–$30	over $30
HOTELS			
under $125	$125–$175	$176–$225	over $225

Tours

★ Full Moon Hike
WALKING TOURS | Rangers lead guided hikes on the nights around each full moon (two per month). You must wear heavy-traction shoes and reserve a spot on the day of the hike. In peak season the tickets are distributed through a lottery system. Schedules are posted at the visitor center and on the park's website. No flash-lights or head lamps are allowed, and children must be at least 8 years old. In winter, when there's at least 16 inches of snow, the hike is by snowshoe. ⊠ *Bryce Canyon National Park* ☎ *435/834–5322* ⊕ *www.nps.gov/brca/planyourvisit/fullmoonhikes.htm.*

Rim Walk

WALKING TOURS | Join a park ranger for a ½-mile, 75-minute-long stroll along the gorgeous rim of Bryce Canyon starting at the Sunset Point overlook. Reservations are not required for the walk, which is offered twice daily from Memorial Day through Labor Day weekends, then usually daily the rest of the year. In winter, when snow levels allow, this becomes a snowshoe hike (for ages 8 and up only). Check with the visitor center or the park website for details. ⊠ *Bryce Canyon National Park* ⊕ *www.nps.gov/brca/planyourvisit/ranger-programs.htm.*

Ruby's Guided ATV Tours

ADVENTURE TOURS | Adventure seekers can take to the trails above the rim on ATVs from late-March through October, weather permitting. A local guide leads the way. Drivers need to be licensed and at least 16 years old and accompanied by an adult if under 18. Passengers must be at least 7 years old. ATVs carry from two to six people, including the driver. Wear long pants or jeans and closed-toed shoes; all other gear is provided. ⊠ *Bryce Canyon Auto Care Center, 105 S. Main St., Bryce Canyon City* ⊹ *Rides depart from the service station* ☎ *435/834–5231* ⊕ *www.rubysinn.com/activities-in-bryce-canyon/guided-atv-tours* 🎫 *From $75.*

Visitor Information

CONTACTS Bryce Canyon National Park. ☎ *435/834–5322* ⊕ *www.nps.gov/brca.*

Bryce Amphitheater

Here at the central part of the park, you'll find the visitor center, lodge, campgrounds, and many of the most popular trails and viewpoints. A convenient free shuttle runs a loop through this area, stopping at eight main spots where you can get out and explore. It also runs through the nearby town of Bryce Canyon City, so you don't need to bring your vehicle if you're staying at one of the hotels just outside the park.

Sights

HISTORICAL SIGHTS

Bryce Canyon Lodge

BUILDING | The lodge's architect, Gilbert Stanley Underwood, was a national park specialist, having designed lodges at Zion and the

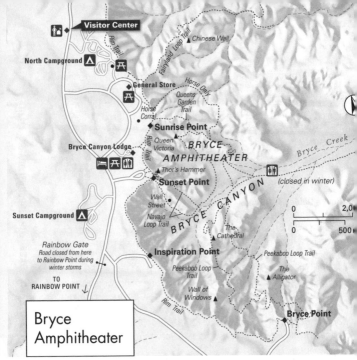

Bryce Amphitheater

Grand Canyon before turning his T square to Bryce in 1924. The results are worth a visit as this National Historic Landmark has been faithfully restored, right down to the lobby's huge limestone fireplace and log and wrought-iron chandelier. Inside the historic building, the only remaining hotel built by the Grand Circle Utah Parks Company, are a restaurant and gift shop, as well as information on park activities. The lodge operation includes several historic log cabins and two motels nearby on the wooded grounds, just a short walk from the rim trail. Everything but the Sunset Lodge (which is open early March–early January) shuts down from early November through late March. ⊠ *Off Hwy. 63, Bryce Canyon National Park* ☎ *435/834–8700* ⊕ *www.brycecanyonforever.com*.

PICNIC AREAS

North Campground Picnic Area

LOCAL INTEREST | This area amid many ponderosa pines has picnic tables and grills usable by non-campers. ⊠ *Main Park Rd., Bryce Canyon National Park* ✛ *Approx. ¼ mile south of Bryce Canyon National Park Visitor Center.*

SCENIC DRIVES
★ Main Park Road
SCENIC DRIVE | Following miles of canyon rim, this thoroughfare gives access to more than a dozen scenic overlooks between the park entrance and Rainbow Point. Major overlooks are rarely more than a few minutes' walk from the parking areas, and many let you see more than 100 miles on clear days. Remember that all overlooks lie east of the road. To keep things simple, proceed to the southern end of the park and stop at the overlooks on your northbound return; they will all be on the right side of the road. Allow two to three hours to travel the entire 36-mile round-trip. The road is open year-round, but may close temporarily after heavy snowfalls. Keep your eyes open for wildlife as you drive. Trailers are not allowed at Bryce Point and Paria View, but you can park them at the parking lot across the road from the visitor center. RVs can drive throughout the park (with limited parking options spring through fall), but vehicles longer than 25 feet are not allowed at Paria View. ✉ Bryce Canyon National Park.

Scenic Byway 12
SCENIC DRIVE | At Red Canyon, 17 miles west of Bryce, a red-rock tunnel (maximum clearance: 13' 6') serves as the unofficial entrance to this delightful, winding, 124-mile journey through some of Utah's most rugged and dramatic landscape. Also to the west, the Tropic Reservoir (the reservoir is west of Bryce, but the town is east of the park) has some of the area's best fishing. To the east, it's 22 miles to Cannonville and one of four Grand Staircase–Escalante National Monument visitor centers. Close by is Kodachrome Basin, a colorful, truly photogenic, moonlike landscape. Ten rough dirt-road miles beyond Kodachrome (go only during dry weather) lies one of Utah's most majestic and tallest arches: Grosvenor. Escalante Petrified Forest State Park is about 50 miles east of Bryce, with dinosaur and flora fossils. ✉ Bryce Canyon National Park.

SCENIC STOPS
Bryce Point
VIEWPOINT | After absorbing views of the Black Mountains and Navajo Mountain, you can follow the Under-the-Rim Trail and go exploring beyond Bryce Amphitheater to the cluster of top-heavy hoodoos known collectively as the Hat Shop. Or, take a left off the Under-the-Rim Trail and hike the challenging Peekaboo Loop Trail with its geological highlight, the Wall of Windows. Openings carved into a wall of rock illustrate the drama of erosion that formed Bryce Canyon. ✉ Inspiration Point Rd., 5½ miles south of park entrance, Bryce Canyon National Park.

The arch tunnel at Red Canyon serves as an "entrance" to the 124-mile Scenic Byway 12.

Fairyland Point

VIEWPOINT | Best visited as you exit the park, this scenic overlook adjacent to Boat Mesa, ½ mile north of the visitor center and a mile off the main park road, has splendid views of Fairyland Amphitheater and its delicate, fanciful forms. The Sinking Ship and other formations stand before the grand backdrop of the Aquarius Plateau and distant Navajo Mountain. Nearby is the Fairyland Loop trailhead—it's a stunning five-hour hike in summer and a favorite of snowshoers in winter. ✉ *Off Hwy. 63, Bryce Canyon National Park.*

★ Inspiration Point

VIEWPOINT | Not far (1½ miles) east along the Rim Trail from Bryce Point is Inspiration Point, site of a wonderful vista on the main amphitheater and one of the best places in the park to see the sunset. (You will have plenty of company and hear a variety of languages as the sun goes down.) ✉ *Inspiration Point Rd., Bryce Canyon National Park* ⊕ *www.nps.gov/brca/planyourvisit/inspiration.htm.*

Mossy Cave

CAVE | Follow the short, well-marked trail of the same name alongside a tranquil brook (except during rare flash floods) and be rewarded with a cave, small waterfall, and some hoodoos. ✉ *Bryce Canyon National Park* ✛ *4 miles east of the junction of Rte. 63 and Hwy. 12.*

Bryce Canyon Geology

It's hard to imagine a prehistoric freshwater lake covering much of Utah and the southwest, but geologists are certain of its former presence. More than 65 million years ago, a network of rivers carried a variety of sediments including iron (yellow and red) and manganese (pink and violet), combining with calcium carbonate (cream) to create Bryce's signature colored limestone. This 1,300-foot deep layer is known as the Claron Formation.

Less than 15 million years ago, an uplift in the Colorado Plateau created a series of smaller plateaus, including the Paunsaugunt (the "rim" of Bryce Canyon) and Table Cliffs (the stunning formation visible as you look east). Water then shaped Bryce's accelerated erosion, not by its volume (a mere 18 inches of precipitation annually) but by the freezing and thawing that takes place more than 200 nights per year.

Finally, streams of water trickle down Bryce's rim forming gullies, cutting deep, narrow channels (called fins) into walls of rock. The fins develop windows, which grow larger (like Natural Bridge) until the roof collapses, creating a hoodoo.

North Campground Viewpoint

VIEWPOINT | FAMILY | Across the road and slightly east of the Bryce Canyon Visitor Center, this popular campground has a couple of scenic picnic areas plus a general store and easy trail access. ⊠ *Main park road, Bryce Canyon National Park* ✛ *½ mile south of visitor center.*

★ Sunrise Point

VIEWPOINT | Named for its stunning views at dawn, this overlook a short walk from Bryce Canyon Lodge is one of the park's most popular stops. It's also the trailhead for the Queen's Garden Trail and the Fairyland Loop Trail. You have to descend the Queen's Garden Trail to get a glimpse of the regal Queen Victoria, a hoodoo that appears to sport a crown and glorious full skirt. The trail is popular and marked clearly, but a bit challenging with 350 feet of elevation change. ⊠ *Off Hwy. 63, Bryce Canyon National Park.*

Sunset Point

VIEWPOINT | Watch the late-day sun paint the hoodoos here. You can see Thor's Hammer, a delicate formation similar to a balanced rock, from the rim, but when you hike 550 feet down into the amphitheater on the Navajo Loop Trail, you can walk through

the famous and very popular Wall Street—a deep, shady "slot" canyon. The point is near Bryce Canyon Lodge. ⊠ *Bryce Canyon National Park* ⊕ *www.nps.gov/brca/planyourvisit/sunset.htm.*

TRAILS

Fairyland Loop Trail

TRAIL | Hike into whimsical Fairyland Canyon on this trail that gets more strenuous and less crowded as you progress along its 8 miles. It winds around hoodoos, across trickles of water, and finally to a natural window in the rock at Tower Bridge, 1½ miles from Sunrise Point and 4 miles from Fairyland Point. The pink-and-white badlands and hoodoos surround you the whole way. Don't feel like you have to go the whole distance to make it worthwhile. But if you do, allow at least five hours round-trip with 1,700 feet of elevation change. *Difficult.* ⊠ *Bryce Canyon National Park* ⊹ *Trailheads: at Fairyland Point and Sunrise Point* ⊕ *www.nps.gov/brca/planyourvisit/fairylandloop.htm.*

Mossy Cave Trail

TRAIL | **FAMILY** | This short hike (0.8 mile) has a little bit of everything you might be looking for in Bryce: the sound of rushing water, a small waterfall, a cave, and hoodoos. The trailhead is on Highway 12, north and east of the main entrance. Ironically, the stream along which you hike isn't really a river—it's an irrigation ditch dug almost 100 years ago by Tropic farmers looking to divert water from the Sevier River for agriculture. Since the dig predates the park, the water right-of-way belongs to the farmers. *Easy.* ⊠ *Hwy. 12, Bryce Canyon National Park* ⊹ *Trailhead: 4 miles east of junction with Rte. 63, 7 miles north of park entrance* ⊙ *www.nps.gov/brca/planyourvisit/mossycavetr.htm.*

Navajo Loop Trail

TRAIL | **FAMILY** | One of Bryce's most popular and dramatic attractions is this steep descent via a series of switchbacks leading to Wall Street, a slightly claustrophobic hallway of rock only 20 feet wide in places, with walls 100 feet high. After a walk through the Silent City, the northern end of the trail brings Thor's Hammer into view. A well-marked intersection offers a shorter way back via Two Bridges Trail or continuing on the Queen's Garden Trail to Sunrise Point. For the short version allow at least an hour on this 1½-mile trail with 550 feet of elevation change. *Moderate.* ⊠ *Bryce Canyon National Park* ⊹ *Trailhead: at Sunset Point, near Bryce Canyon Lodge* ⊕ *www.nps.gov/brca/planyourvisit/navajotrail.htm.*

The aptly named Wall of Windows is a highlight of the challenging Peekaboo Loop Trail.

★ Navajo/Queen's Garden Combination Loop

TRAIL | FAMILY | By walking this extended 3-mile loop, you can see some of the best of Bryce; it takes a little more than two hours. The route passes fantastic formations and an open forest of pine and juniper on the amphitheater floor. Descend into the amphitheater from Sunrise Point on the Queen's Garden Trail and ascend via the Navajo Loop Trail; return to your starting point via the Rim Trail. *Moderate.* ⊠ *Bryce Canyon National Park* ⊹ *Trailheads: at Sunset and Sunrise Points, 2 miles south of park entrance* ⊕ *www.nps.gov/brca/planyourvisit/qgnavajocombo.htm.*

★ Peekaboo Loop Trail

TRAIL | The reward of this steep trail is the Wall of Windows and the Three Wise Men. Horses use this trail in spring, summer, and fall and have the right-of-way. Start at Bryce, Sunrise, or Sunset Point and allow four to five hours to hike the 5-mile loop or 7-mile double-loop. *Difficult.* ⊠ *Bryce Canyon National Park* ⊹ *Trailheads: at Bryce Point, 5½ miles south of park entrance; Sunrise and Sunset Points, near Bryce Canyon Lodge.*

★ Queen's Garden Trail

TRAIL | FAMILY | This hike is the easiest way down into the amphitheater, with 350 feet of elevation change leading to a short tunnel, quirky hoodoos, and lots of like-minded hikers. It's the essential Bryce "sampler." Allow two hours total to hike the 1½-mile trail plus the ½-mile rim-side path and back. *Easy.* ⊠ *Bryce Canyon*

Native American History in Bryce

According to Paiute legend, the hoodoos are Legend People, predecessors who were turned to stone by coyotes, some still with paint on their faces.

Human history in Bryce Canyon dates back some 2,000 years to the Ancestral Puebloans, also known as Anasazi. The Fremont people are believed to have lived in the area in the 1200s, followed by the Paiute. According to author Greer Chesher, who's written extensively about Bryce Canyon, the Paiutes depended on springs "in and around Bryce, like piki-pa below Yovimpa Point, which may be what we know today as Riggs Spring." In summer, the Fremont and Paiute cultures would have been attracted by the Bryce rim's pine nuts, sego lily roots, and animals for nourishment.

The 19th-century establishment of 11 Mormon settlements in southern Utah heralded the end of the Paiute relationship with the lands in and around Bryce. Not only did the tribe face competition for land and resources, but it also faced epidemics. Many Paiute lives were lost to disease at this time. Later in the century, those who survived were moved to reservations. They eventually lost not only these lands but also, in the 1950s, their designation as a tribe owing to federal government policies of the time. Even basic health care became an issue: between 1954 and 1980, more than half of the remaining Paiute died. Although recognition of the Paiute as a tribe was restored in 1980, only a fraction of their original reservation lands was returned to them.

National Park ✛ *Trailhead: at Sunrise Point, 2 miles south of park entrance* ⊕ *www.nps.gov/brca/planyourvisit/queensgarden.htm.*

★ Rim Trail

TRAIL | A 1-mile section of the trail connects Sunrise and Sunset points and is an ideal way to launch or wrap up your day. Take your time strolling. Evening may be the best time for photos, as much of the rim looks out to the east over the amphitheater. Listen for songbirds, look for a silent swooping owl, and watch the sun's last rays dance on the hoodoos. This section of the trail is wheelchair accessible, and pets on leashes are welcome. More ambitious walkers will enjoy the full, 5.5-mile trail between Bryce Point and Fairyland Point, which has a few steep elevation changes. *Easy to moderate.* ⊠ *Main Park Rd., Bryce Canyon National Park* ✛ *Trailhead: 2 miles south of park entrance* ⊕ *www.nps.gov/brca/ planyourvisit/rimtrail.htm.*

Did You Know?

Evocatively named formations along the Navajo Loop Trail, which can be combined with the Queen's Garden Trail for a longer hike, include Wall Street, Silent City, and Thor's Hammer.

Tower Bridge

TRAIL | This short, less-crowded hike on the Fairyland Loop Trail takes you to a natural bridge deep in the amphitheater. Walk through pink and white badlands with hoodoos all around on this 3-mile trip that takes two to three hours and has 800 feet of elevation change. It is not in itself a loop trail if you start and return to Sunrise Point rather than continue on the Fairyland Loop. *Moderate.* ☒ *Bryce Canyon National Park* ⊹ *Trailhead: at Sunrise Point, 1 mile off main park road, south of park entrance* ⊕ *www. nps.gov/brca/planyourvisit/towerbridge.htm.*

VISITOR CENTERS

★ Bryce Canyon Visitor Center

INFO CENTER | **FAMILY** | Even if you're anxious to hit the hoodoos, the visitor center—just to your right after the park entrance station—is the best place to start if you want to know what you're looking at and how it got there. Rangers staff a counter where you can ask questions or let them map out an itinerary of "must-sees" based on your time and physical abilities. There are also multimedia exhibits, Wi-Fi, books, maps, backcountry camping permits for sale, and the Bryce Canyon Natural History Association gift shop, whose proceeds help to support park programs and conservation. ☒ *Hwy. 63, Bryce Canyon National Park* ☎ *435/834–5322* ⊕ *www. nps.gov/brca.*

🍴 Restaurants

★ Bryce Canyon Lodge Restaurant

$$$ | **AMERICAN** | With a high-beam ceiling, tall windows, and a massive stone fireplace, the dining room at this historic lodge set among towering pines abounds with rustic western charm. The kitchen serves three meals a day (reservations aren't accepted, so be prepared for a wait), and the dishes—highlights of which include buffalo sirloin steak, burgundy-braised bison stew, and almond-and-panko-crusted trout—feature organic or sustainable ingredients whenever possible. **Known for:** good selection of local craft beers; delicious desserts, including a fudge-brownie sundae and six-layer carrot cake; hearty breakfasts. ⑤ *Average main: $28* ☒ *Off Hwy. 63, Bryce Canyon National Park* ☎ *435/834–8700* ⊕ *www.brycecanyonforever.com/dining* ⊘ *Closed early Nov.–late Mar.*

Valhalla Pizzeria & Coffee Shop

$ | **PIZZA** | **FAMILY** | A quick and casual 40-seat eatery across the parking lot from Bryce Canyon Lodge, this pizzeria and coffee shop is a good bet for an inexpensive meal, especially when the lodge dining room is too crowded. Coffee shop choices include

Plants and Wildlife in Bryce

With elevations approaching 9,000 feet, many of Bryce Canyon's 400 plant species are unlike those you'll see at less lofty places. Look at exposed slopes and you might catch a glimpse of the pygmy pinyon or the gnarled, 1,000-year-old bristlecone pine. At lower altitudes are the Douglas fir, the ponderosa pine, and the quaking aspen, which sit in groves of twinkling leaves. No fewer than three kinds of sagebrush—big, black, and fringed—grow here, as well as the blue columbine.

Mule deer and chipmunks are common companions on the trails and are used to human presence. You might also catch a glimpse of the endangered Utah prairie dog. Give them a wide berth; they may be cute, but they bite (and it's illegal to approach or feed wildlife in any national park). Other animals include elk, black-tailed jackrabbits, and the desert cottontail. More than 210 species of birds live in the park or pass through as a migratory stop. Bird-watchers are often rewarded handsomely for their vigilance: eagles, peregrine falcons, and even the rare California condor have all been spotted in the park.

an espresso bar, housemade pastries, and fresh fruit, or kick back on the tranquil patio in the evening and enjoy fresh pizza or salad. **Known for:** convenient and casual; decent beer and wine selection; filling pizzas. ⑤ *Average main: $13* ⊠ *Off Hwy. 63, Bryce Canyon National Park* ☎ *435/834–8709* ⊕ *www.brycecanyonforever.com/pizza* ☉ *Closed mid-Sept.–mid-May.*

🛏 Hotels

★ Bryce Canyon Lodge
$$$ | HOTEL | This historic, rugged stone-and-wood lodge close to the amphitheater's rim offers western-style rooms with semi-private balconies or porches in two motel buildings; suites in the historic inn; and cozy, beautifully designed lodgepole pine-and-stone cabins, some with cathedral ceilings and gas fireplaces.
Pros: close to canyon rim and trails; lodge is steeped in history and has loads of personality; cabins have fireplaces and exude rustic charm. **Cons:** closed in winter; books up fast; no TVs or air-conditioning. ⑤ *Rooms from: $223* ⊠ *Off Hwy. 63, Bryce Canyon National Park* ☎ *435/834–8700, 877/386–4383* ⊕ *www.brycecanyonforever.com* ☉ *Closed Jan.–early Mar.* ⇥ *113 rooms* ⑩ *No meals.*

Although short (1½ miles), the "easiest" route down into the amphitheater takes two hours.

 ## Shopping

Bryce Canyon General Store

CONVENIENCE/GENERAL STORES | Buy groceries, T-shirts, hats, books, postcards, and camping items that you might have left behind, as well as snacks, drinks, juices, and quick meals at this multipurpose facility at Sunrise Point near the North Campground. Picnic tables under pine trees offer a shady break. ⊠ *Bryce Canyon National Park* ✛ *About ½ mile off the main park road, 2 miles south of the park entrance* ☎ ⊕ *www.brycecanyonforever.com/ bryce-canyon-shopping* ☉ *Closed Nov.–mid-Mar.*

Bryce Canyon Lodge Gift Shop

CONVENIENCE/GENERAL STORES | Here you can buy Native American and Southwestern crafts, such as pottery and jewelry, along with T-shirts, jackets, dolls, and books. ⊠ *Bryce Canyon Lodge, Hwy. 63, 2 miles south of park entrance, Bryce Canyon National Park* ☎ *435/834–8700* ⊕ *www.brycecanyonforever.com/bryce-can- yon-shopping* ☉ *Closed mid-Nov.–late Mar.*

Visitor Center Bookstore

BOOKS/STATIONERY | The Bryce Canyon Natural History Association runs a bookstore inside the park visitor center where you can find maps, books, videos, stuffed animals, DVDs, clothing, and postcards. ⊠ *Bryce Canyon Visitor Center, 1 mile south of park entrance, Bryce Canyon National Park* ☎ *888/362–2642* ⊕ *www. shop.brycecanyon.org.*

Under-the-Rim

Bryce Canyon's longest trail leads backpackers under the rim of the park's plateau that edges the natural amphitheater. Hiking the full 23-mile Under-the-Rim Trail will require an overnight stay, though there are some shorter trails to access parts of this area on day hikes. On clear nights, the stargazing can be amazing.

Sights

PICNIC AREAS

Whiteman Bench

LOCAL INTEREST | There are picnic tables here at this trailhead for the Swamp Canyon portion of the Under-the-Rim Trail. The views aren't spectacular even though you're atop the Pink Cliffs portion of the canyon. It's ideally located for a quick break during your start-and-stop drive. ⊠ *Main Park Rd., Bryce Canyon National Park* ✛ *10 miles south of the park entrance.*

SCENIC STOPS

Agua Canyon

VIEWPOINT | This overlook in the southern section of the park, 12 miles south of the park entrance, has a nice view of several stand-out hoodoos. Look for the top-heavy formation called the Hunter, which actually has a few small hardy trees growing on its cap. As the rock erodes, the park evolves; snap a picture because the Hunter may look different the next time you visit. ⊠ *Bryce Canyon National Park* ⊕ *www.nps.gov/brca/planyourvisit/aguacanyon.htm.*

Natural Bridge

VIEWPOINT | Formed over millions of years by wind, water, and chemical erosion, this 85-foot rusty-orange arch formation—one of several rock arches in the park—is an essential photo op. Beyond the parking lot lies a rare stand of aspen trees, their leaves twinkling in the wind. Watch out for distracted drivers at this stunning viewpoint. ⊠ *Main park road, 11 miles south of park entrance, Bryce Canyon National Park* ⊕ *www.nps.gov/brca/planyourvisit/naturalbridge.htm.*

Paria View

VIEWPOINT | Gaze into the Paria River watershed below in a unique southwest-facing overlook. Far below you, hardy hikers on the Under-the-Rim Trail may be refilling their supplies at the lush, green Yellow Creek Meadow. Also, look for mule deer, elk, and pronghorn in the meadows near here—and peregrine falcons nesting or hunting along the cliffs. Skiers love this 3.5-mile cross-country loop in winter. ✉ *Off Bryce Point Rd., Bryce Canyon National Park* ✛ *7½ miles south of the park entrance* ⊕ *www.nps. gov/brca/planyourvisit/paria.htm.*

Piracy Point

VIEWPOINT | A gallery of views, this primitive picnic area lies ¼ mile north of Farview Point, slightly off the main road. ✉ *About 8 miles south of the park entrance on the main park road, Bryce Canyon National Park.*

TRAILS

Hat Shop Trail

TRAIL | The sedimentary haberdashery sits 2 miles from the trail-head. Hard gray caps balance precariously atop narrow pedestals of softer, rust-color rock. Allow three to four hours to travel this somewhat strenuous but rewarding 4-mile round-trip trail, the first part of the longer Under-the-Rim Trail. *Moderate.* ✉ *Bryce Canyon National Park* ✛ *Trailhead: at Bryce Point, 5½ miles south of park entrance* ⊕ *www.nps.gov/brca/planyourvisit/hatshop.htm.*

Under-the-Rim Trail

TRAIL | Starting at Bryce Point, the trail travels 23 miles to Rainbow Point, passing through the Pink Cliffs, traversing Agua Canyon and Ponderosa Canyon, and taking you by several springs. Most of the hike is on the amphitheater floor, characterized by up-and-down terrain among stands of ponderosa pine; the elevation change totals about 1,500 feet. It's the park's longest trail, but four trail-heads along the main park road allow you to connect to the Under-the-Rim Trail and cover its length as a series of day hikes. Allow at least two days to hike the route in its entirety, and although it's not a hoodoo-heavy hike, there's plenty to see to make it a more leisurely three-day affair. *Difficult.* ✉ *Bryce Canyon National Park* ✛ *Trailheads: at Bryce Point, Swamp Canyon, Ponderosa Canyon, and Rainbow Point.*

Rainbow and Yovimpa Points

Heading south from the park entrance, this is as far as you can drive on the 18-mile park road. The area includes a short, easy trail through the forest as well as a longer difficult trail. The viewpoints at Rainbow and Yovimpa look to the north and south, so you'll want to visit both. Many visitors like to drive to this part of the park first, and then drive back north.

Sights

PICNIC AREAS
Yovimpa Point Picnic Area
LOCAL INTEREST | At the southern end of the park, this shady, quiet spot looks out onto the 100-mile vistas from the rim. There are tables and restrooms. ⊠ *Main Park Rd., Bryce Canyon National Park* ✛ *18 miles south of Bryce Canyon National Park entrance.*

SCENIC DRIVES AND STOPS
★ Rainbow and Yovimpa Points
VIEWPOINT | Separated by less than half a mile, Rainbow and Yovimpa points offer two fine panoramas facing opposite directions. Rainbow Point's best view is to the north overlooking the southern rim of the amphitheater and giving a glimpse of Grand Staircase–Escalante National Monument; Yovimpa Point's vista spreads out to the south. On an especially clear day you can see all the way to Arizona's highest point, Humphrey's Peak, 150 miles away. Yovimpa Point also has a shady and quiet picnic area with tables and restrooms. You can hike between them on the easy Bristlecone Loop Trail or tackle the more strenuous 9-mile Riggs Spring Loop Trail, which passes the tallest point in the park. This is the outermost auto stop on the main road, so visitors often drive here first and make it their starting point, then work their way back to the park entrance. ⊠ *End of main park road, 18 miles south of park entrance, Bryce Canyon National Park.*

TRAILS
Bristlecone Loop Trail
TRAIL | This 1-mile trail with a modest 200 feet of elevation gain lets you see the park from its highest points of more than 9,000 feet, alternating between spruce and fir forest and wide-open vistas out over Grand Staircase–Escalante National Monument and beyond. You might see yellow-bellied marmots and dusky grouse,

Yovimpa Point Overlook has a shady picnic area and 100-mile vistas.

critters not found at lower elevations in the park. Plan on 45 minutes to an hour. *Easy.* ⊠ *Bryce Canyon National Park* ✛ *Trailhead: at Rainbow Point parking lot, 18 miles south of park entrance* ⊕ *www.nps.gov/brca/planyourvisit/bristleconeloop.htm.*

Riggs Spring Loop Trail

TRAIL | One of the park's two true backpacker trails, this rigorous 9-mile path has overnight options at three campsites along the way. You'll journey past groves of twinkling aspen trees and the eponymous spring close to the campsite. Start at either Yovimpa or Rainbow Point and be prepared for 1,500 feet of elevation change. Campers need to check in at the visitor center ahead of time for backcountry permits. *Difficult.* ⊠ *Bryce Canyon National Park* ✛ *Trailheads: at Yovimpa and Rainbow points, 18 miles south of park entrance* ⊕ *www.nps.gov/brca/planyourvisit/riggsspringloop.htm.*

Bryce Canyon City

Right outside the park, this village has several lodging and dining options, shops, gas, tourist attractions, and other helpful amenities for park visitors. The park shuttle bus makes several stops in the town.

Sights

MUSEUMS

Bryce Wildlife Adventure

MUSEUM | FAMILY | Imagine a zoo frozen in time: this 14,000-square-foot private museum contains more than 1,600 butterflies and 1,000 taxidermy animals in tableaux mimicking actual terrain and animal behavior. The animals and birds come from all parts of the world. An African room has baboons, bush pigs, Cape buffalo, and a lion. There's also a collection of living deer that kids delight in feeding, and ATV and bike rentals for touring scenic Highway 12 and the Paunsaugunt Plateau. ⊠ *1945 W. Hwy. 12, Bryce Canyon City* ☎ *435/834–5555* ⊕ *www.brycewildlifeadventure.com* 🎟 *$8* ⊗ *Closed mid-Nov.–Mar.*

SCENIC DRIVES

U.S. 89/Utah's Heritage Highway

SCENIC DRIVE | Winding north from the Arizona border all the way to Spanish Fork Canyon, an hour south of Salt Lake City, U.S. 89 is known as the Heritage Highway for its role in shaping Utah history. At its southern end, Kanab is known as "Little Hollywood," having provided the backdrop for many famous Western movies and TV commercials. Other towns north along this famous road may not have the same notoriety in these parts, but they do offer eye-popping scenery as well as some lodging and dining options relatively close to Bryce Canyon.

🍴 Restaurants

Bryce Canyon Pines Restaurant

$$ | AMERICAN | Inside the Bryce Canyon Pines Motel, about 6 miles northwest of Bryce Canyon National Park, this down-home, family-friendly roadhouse decorated with Old West photos and memorabilia serves reliably good stick-to-your-ribs breakfasts, hefty elk burgers, rib-eye steaks, and Utah rainbow trout. But the top draw here is homemade pie, which comes in a vast assortment of flavors, from banana-blueberry cream to boysenberry. **Known for:** delectable pies; friendly staff; plenty of kids' options. 💲 *Average main: $16* ⊠ *Hwy. 12, mile marker 10, Bryce Canyon City* ☎ *435/834–5441* ⊕ *www.brycecanyonrestaurant.com.*

Hotels

Best Western Bryce Canyon Grand Hotel
$$$ | **HOTEL** | If you appreciate creature comforts but can do without much in the way of local personality, this four-story hotel just outside the park fits the bill—rooms are relatively posh, with comfortable mattresses, pillows, and bedding, spacious bathrooms, and modern appliances, and there's an outdoor pool and pleasant patio. **Pros:** clean, spacious rooms; lots of amenities and activities; short drive or free shuttle ride from Bryce Canyon. **Cons:** no pets allowed; pricey during busy times; standard chain ambience. ⑤ *Rooms from: $220* ⊠ *30 N. 100 E, Bryce Canyon City* ☎ *866/866–6634, 435/834–5700* ⊕ *www.brycecanyongrand. com* ⇱ *164 rooms* ⦿ *Free breakfast.*

Best Western Plus Ruby's Inn
$$$ | **HOTEL** | **FAMILY** | This bustling Southwestern-themed hotel has expanded over the years to include various wings with rooms that vary widely in terms of size and character. **Pros:** lots of services and amenities; short drive or free shuttle ride into the park; nice indoor pool. **Cons:** can get very busy, especially when the big tour buses roll in; too big for charm or a quiet getaway; uneven quality of restaurants. ⑤ *Rooms from: $190* ⊠ *26 S. Main St., Bryce Canyon City* ☎ *435/834–5341, 866/866–6616* ⊕ *www.rubysinn.com* ⇱ *368 rooms* ⦿ *Free breakfast.*

Bryce Canyon Pines Motel
$$ | **HOTEL** | Most rooms in this motel complex tucked into the woods 6 miles southwest of the park entrance have excellent mountain views. **Pros:** guided horseback rides; outdoor pool and hot tub; lively restaurant famed for homemade pies. **Cons:** thin walls; room quality varies widely; furnishings are a bit dated. ⑤ *Rooms from: $125* ⊠ *Hwy. 12, mile marker 10, Bryce Canyon City* ☎ *435/834–5441* ⊕ *www.brycecanyonmotel.com* ⇱ *46 rooms* ⦿ *No meals.*

Shopping

Ruby's General Store
CONVENIENCE/GENERAL STORES | It may not be one of the area's geological wonders, but this giant mercantile center almost has to be seen to be believed. On a busy evening, it bustles with tourists plucking through souvenirs that range from sweatshirts to wind chimes. There are also selections of Western wear, children's toys, holiday gifts, and groceries. Even the camping equipment is in ample supply. Need a folding stove, sleeping bag, or fishing gear?

Bryce Point

Paria View

BRYCE CANYON
NATIONAL PARK

Sheep Creek
Connecting Trail

PINK CLIFFS

Under-the-Rim
Trail

Swamp Canyon

Swamp Canyon
Connecting Trail

▲ Swamp Canyon Butte

▲ Mud Canyon Butte

MUD CANYON

Noon
Canyon Butte ▲

NOON CANYON

Whiteman
Connecting
Trail

Piracy Point

Farview Point

DIXIE
NATIONAL
FOREST

Natural Bridge

BRIDGE CANYON

PINK CLIFFS

Deer
Mountain ▲

Horse
Mountain ▲

**Agua
Canyon**

AGUA CYN.

Agua Canyon
Connecting Trail

Under-the-Rim
Trail

Under-the-Rim
Trail

**Ponderosa
Canyon**

**Black Birch
Canyon**

**Rainbow
Point**

▲ The Promontory

Yovimpa Point

Twin
Hills ▲

Bristlecone Loop
Trail

Riggs Spring
Trail

PINK CLIFFS

MUTTON HOLLOW

Southern
Bryce Canyon

0 ——— 1 mi

0 ——— 1 km

You will find it at Ruby's. You can also cross Main Street to where this ever-expanding complex has added a line of shops trimmed like an Old West town, complete with candy store and rock shop. ✉ *26 S. Main St., Bryce Canyon National Park* ☎ *435/834–5484* ⊕ *www.rubysinn.com/rubys-inn-store.*

Activities

Most visitors explore Bryce Canyon by car, but the hiking trails are far more rewarding. At these elevations, you'll have to stop to catch your breath more often if you're used to being closer to sea level. It gets warm in summer but rarely uncomfortably hot, so hiking farther into the depths of the park is not difficult, so long as you don't pick a hike that is beyond your abilities.

Air Tours

Bryce Canyon Airlines & Helicopters

TOUR—SPORTS | For a bird's-eye view of Bryce Canyon National Park, take a dramatic helicopter ride or airplane tour over the fantastic sandstone formations. Longer full-canyon tours and added excursions to sites such as the Grand Canyon, Monument Valley, and Zion are also offered. Flights last from 35 minutes to four hours. ☎ *435/834–8060* ⊕ *www.rubysinn.com/scenic-flights* 🖃 *From $110.*

Biking

Riding inside Bryce Canyon will not be the easiest 40 miles in your life (20 miles each way from Ruby's Inn to Rainbow Point), but it certainly is a great workout. It's not traffic free, either, but if you hit the road at dawn you'll have a lot of road to yourself. Officially, the elevation gain from north to south is only about 1,200 feet, but when you're going from 7,890 feet (above sea level) to 9,110 feet, your body is really going to feel it. There are some radical curving descents along the way, which only lead to more climbing … and more climbing. For an easier go, have a friend drive you to Rainbow Point and bike back to the entrance one-way.

Mountain bike or hybrid riders should pay heed to the Great Western Trail, which bisects Route 63 between Ruby's Inn and the Fairyland Point turnout. Open to bikes, four-wheelers, horses, and (in winter) snowmobiles, the trail can be followed for up to about

400 miles across Utah alone. The full trail, which includes many hiking-only sections, connects Mexico and Canada.

Ruby's Inn Mountain Bike Rentals

BICYCLING | Ruby's Inn rents mountain bikes for $10 per hour, $25 per half-day, and $40 daily for full-day or longer excursions. The hotel can also recommend single-track trails in the surrounding region (bikes are not allowed off-road in the park). ⊠ *105 S. Main St., Bryce Canyon City* ☏ *435/834–5231* ⊕ *www.rubysinn.com/ mountain-bike-rentals.*

Bird-Watching

More than 210 bird species have been identified in Bryce. Violet-green swallows and white-throated swifts are common, as are Steller's jays, American coots, rufous hummingbirds, and mountain bluebirds. Lucky bird-watchers will see golden eagles floating across the skies above the pink rocks of the amphitheater, and experienced birders might spot an osprey nest high in the canyon wall. The best time in the park for avian variety is from May through July.

Camping

Campgrounds in Bryce Canyon are family-friendly and drive-in, except for the handful of backcountry sites that only backpackers and gung-ho day hikers ever see. Most campgrounds are first-come, first-served in high season. That said, call and check about making reservations; slots fill up fast, particularly in summer, so book ahead when you can. Tent sites are $20 per night; RV sites are $30.

Most of the area's state parks have camping facilities, and Dixie National Forest contains many wonderful sites. Campgrounds may close seasonally (one loop of North Campground remains open year-round), and roads may occasionally close in winter while heavy snow is cleared.

IN THE PARK

North Campground. A cool, shady retreat in a forest of ponderosa pines, this is a great home base for campers visiting Bryce Canyon. You're near the general store, the Lodge, trailheads, and the visitor center. Sites are first-come, first-served, and the campground usually fills by early afternoon in July, August, and September. Just be aware that some sites feel crowded and un-private.

✉ *Main park road, ½ mile south of visitor center* ☎ *435/834–5322*
🏕 *49 RV sites, 59 tent sites.*

Sunset Campground. This serene, alpine campground is within walking distance of Bryce Canyon Lodge and many trailheads. Sites can be reserved up to six months in advance for the peak season; in the shoulder season, they're available first-come, first-served. The campground fills by early afternoon in July though September, so secure your campsite before you sightsee. Reservations are required for the group site. As one of the most accessible hiking areas of the park, it can be crowded. This campground is closed from November through mid-April. ✉ *Main park road, 2 miles south of visitor center* ☎ *435/834–5322* ⊕ *www.recreation.gov* 🏕 *100 sites (50 for RVs).*

IN BRYCE CANYON CITY

Bryce Canyon Pines Campground and RV Park. This campground, 6 miles from the park entrance, is shady and quiet. It's on the grounds of Bryce Canyon Pines Motel and has showers and a guest laundry. ✉ *Rte. 12, 6 miles northwest of the park entrance, Bryce Canyon City* ☎ *435/834–5441* ⊕ *www.brycecanyonmotel. com/bryce-campgrounds* 🏕 *18 tent sites, 30 RV sites, 1 group site.*

Ruby's Inn Campground and RV Park. Just a mile north of the entrance to Bryce Canyon National Park, this large campground spreads out a few steps from the Ruby's complex. Most of the campsites are in an open area, with full hook-ups or electricity and water; there are also tent sites, group camping sites, and rustic teepees and cabins beneath the pine and fir trees that surround the RV park. The campground has plenty of amenities, including a seasonal outdoor pool, laundry facilities, and showers. ✉ *20 S. Main St., Bryce Canyon City* ☎ *866–878–9373, 435/834–5341* ⊕ *www.brycecanyoncampgrounds.com* 🏕 *243 sites.*

Educational Programs

RANGER PROGRAMS
Campfire and Auditorium Programs
TOUR—SIGHT | FAMILY | Bryce Canyon's natural diversity comes alive in the park's North Campground amphitheater, the Visitor Center Theater, or the Bryce Canyon Lodge Auditorium. Ranger talks, multimedia programs, and guided walks introduce you to geology, astronomy, wildlife, history, and many other topics related to Bryce Canyon and the West. ✉ *Bryce Canyon National Park* ⊕ *www.nps.gov/brca/planyourvisit/ranger-programs.htm.*

Geology Talks

TOUR—SIGHT | FAMILY | Rangers host free 20-minute discussions twice a day about the long geological history of Bryce Canyon. These interesting talks are held at Sunset Point. No reservations are needed. ✉ *Bryce Canyon National Park* ⊕ *www.nps.gov/brca/planyourvisit/ranger-programs.htm.*

Junior Ranger Program

TOUR—SIGHT | FAMILY | Kids can sign up to be Junior Rangers at the Bryce Canyon Visitor Center. They have to complete several activities in their free Junior Ranger booklet and attend a ranger program, visit the park museum, or watch the park movie. Allow three to six hours total to earn the park's Junior Ranger badge. Ask a ranger about each day's schedule of events and topics, or look for postings at the visitor center and Bryce Canyon Lodge or on campground bulletin boards. ✉ *Bryce Canyon National Park* ⊕ *www.nps.gov/brca/learn/kidsyouth/beajuniorranger.htm.*

Telescopes Program

TOUR—SIGHT | FAMILY | City folk are lucky to see 2,500 stars in their artificially illuminated skies, but out here among the hoodoos you see three times as many. The 90-minute program at the visitor center includes low-key ranger talks on astronomy, followed by telescope viewing (weather permitting). The program is typically offered on Thursday–Saturday nights at 10 pm from Memorial Day through Labor Day weekends and some Saturdays during the rest of the year. Check at the visitor center for details. ✉ *Bryce Canyon National Park* ⊕ *www.nps.gov/brca/planyourvisit/ranger-programs.htm.*

Hiking

There's a pattern to hikes in Bryce—start at the rim, descend into the canyon, explore among the red rocks, then climb out. Because of the need to regain distance at the end of virtually every hiking trail in the park, all of these hikes will be moderately strenuous. To reach the hoodoos (caused by erosion, freezing, and thawing of the rim of a cliff), you'll have to endure steep and often uneven trails. Remember that bighorn sheep are more naturally inclined to this landscape than humans.

But if you want to get up close and personal with these wondrous formations, set aside at least a half-day for a hike. If you have time for just one trail, choose the Navajo Loop/Queen's Garden combination. With a little more time, pick one of the outlying hikes: Fairyland Point, the Hat Shop, or Riggs Springs (which has backcountry campsites, but, since it's a 9-mile hike, many prefer to do it in one day).

One of the smallest national parks by area, Bryce Canyon does not have as much backcountry as, say, the Grand Canyon or Zion. The 23-mile Under-the-Rim Trail is the primary backcountry option. Situated almost entirely at the base of the canyon, it might be the only place where hikers could get lost in the woods and encounter bears and mountain lions. Allow at least two days to hike the length of the trail in either direction. For a shorter version, drop down to the trail at any of four connecting trails (perhaps Swamp Canyon or Whiteman Bench) along the park road. You'll need to arrange a pickup or dropoff, as the park shuttle service does not cover the full length of the park.

Utah Prairie Dog

Bryce Canyon National Park reintroduced the Utah prairie dog (*Cynomys parvidens*) to its meadows during the 1970s and 1980s. Numbering approximately 200 in Bryce today (and less than 5,000 across the southwest portion of the state), the Utah prairie dog was initially protected under the Endangered Species Act in 1973, with its status improving slightly from "endangered" to "threatened" a decade later. Bryce is the only National Park Service unit where these creatures are found.

The uneven terrain calls for sturdy hiking boots. In summer, consider hiking in the morning to avoid the day's warmest temperatures and strongest sun. Keep in mind that if you're not used to exercising at elevation, you can fall victim to altitude sickness. For trail maps, information, and ranger recommendations, stop at the park's visitor center. Bathrooms are at most trailheads but not down in the amphitheater.

Horseback Riding

Few activities conjure up the Old West like riding a horse, and Bryce Canyon offers plenty of opportunities to see the sights from the saddle. Many of the park's hiking trails were first formed beneath the hooves of cattle wranglers, and their modern-day counterparts now guide tourists over these and other trails. Canyon Trail Rides is the only outfitter with permission to conduct rides in the park. Several area outfitters offer rides in the surrounding Dixie National Forest and Grand Staircase–Escalante National Monument. Minimum rider age and maximum rider weight vary

Get a taste of the Old West on a horseback ride through Bryce Canyon.

according to the chosen ride (anywhere from a half-hour to a full day or more in length), but typically those under the age of 7 and over the weight of 230 pounds are prohibited.

Canyon Trail Rides

HORSEBACK RIDING | FAMILY | Descend to the floor of the Bryce Canyon Amphitheater via horse or mule—most visitors have no riding experience, so don't hesitate to join in. A two-hour ride (children as young as 7 can participate) ambles along the amphitheater floor through the Queen's Garden before returning to Sunrise Point. The three-hour expedition (children must be at least 10 years old) follows Peekaboo Loop Trail, winds past the Fairy Castle, and passes the Wall of Windows before returning to Sunrise Point. For either ride, the weight limit is 220 pounds. Two rides a day of each type leave in the morning and early afternoon. There are no rides from November through March. ⊠ *Bryce Canyon Lodge, Off Hwy. 63, Bryce Canyon National Park* ☎ *435/679–8665, 435/834–5500 Bryce Canyon reservations* ⊕ *www.canyonrides.com* ✉ *From $65.*

Ruby's Horseback Adventures

HORSEBACK RIDING | FAMILY | Ride to the rim of Bryce Canyon, venture through narrow slot canyons in Grand Staircase–Escalante National Monument, or even retrace the trails taken by outlaw Butch Cassidy more than a century ago. Rides last from 90 minutes to all day. Kids must be 7 or older to ride, in some cases 10. Wagon rides to the rim of Bryce Canyon are available for all ages, as are sleigh rides in winter. ⊠ *Bryce Canyon National Park* ☎ *866/782–0002* ⊕ *www.horserides.net* ✉ *From $68.*

Winter Activities

Unlike most of Utah's other national parks, Bryce Canyon receives plenty of snow, making it a popular cross-country ski area. Rim Trail, Paria Loop, and other paths above the canyon are popular destinations. The visitor center sells shoe-traction devices, and some of the ranger-guided snowshoe activities include snowshoes and poles.

Ruby's Winter Activities Center

SKIING/SNOWBOARDING | FAMILY | This facility grooms miles of private, no-cost trails that connect to the ungroomed trails inside the park. Rental snowshoes, ice skates, and cross-country ski equipment are available. ⊠ *Hwy. 63, 1 mile north of park entrance, Bryce Canyon City* ☎ *435/834–5341, 866/866–6616* ⊕ *www. rubysinn.com/winter-activities.*

BRYCE CANYON GATEWAYS

Updated by
Shelley Arenas

⊙ **Sights**   🍴 **Restaurants**   🛏 **Hotels**   🛍 **Shopping**   🍸 **Nightlife**

★★★★★   ★★★★☆   ★★★★☆   ★★★★☆   ★★★★☆

WELCOME TO BRYCE CANYON GATEWAYS

TOP REASONS TO GO

★ **A wild ride:** Spectacular Highway 12 snakes its way to Grand Staircase–Escalante National Monument.

★ **Shakespeare on high:** Watch plays by the bard during Cedar City's Utah Shakespeare Festival.

★ **Altitude action:** Brian Head's resort offers skiing, snowboarding, mountain biking, and hiking.

★ **Epic stargazing:** Cedar Breaks National Monument has become a center of astro-tourism.

1 Panguitch. Count on this low-key town for inexpensive, casual lodgings and eateries within striking distance of Bryce Canyon and Cedar Breaks.

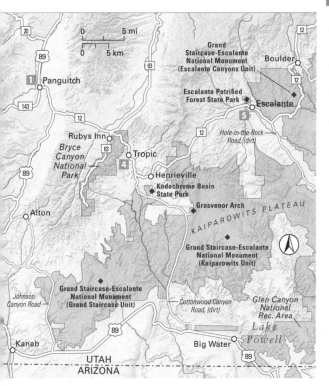

2 Brian Head. The state's southernmost ski town is the nearest base for exploring Cedar Breaks.

3 Cedar City. The home of Southern Utah University has many cultural draws, including the Utah Shakespeare Festival.

4 Tropic. Tiny Tropic is handy for visiting Bryce Canyon.

5 Escalante. This picturesque village on Highway 12 is a recreation hub.

Several cool—literally, given the altitude, and figuratively—towns make great bases for exploring Bryce Canyon National Park. To the west are Panguitch, a pioneer town; the resort town of Brian Head; and Cedar City, home to a university. To the east are tiny Tropic, just outside the park, and Escalante.

Both Panguitch and Brian Head are also ideal bases for exploring Cedar Breaks National Monument, an International Dark Sky Park with many astronomy programs. In recent years, it was singled out by readers of a national daily newspaper for offering the "best national park night experience." Set at 10,000 feet, in cold months, Cedar Breaks is generally accessible only by snowshoes, skis, or snowmobiles. Likewise, some of the services in Panguitch close seasonally—at an elevation of over 6,600 feet, winters here are snowy. In fact, during the harsh winter of 1864, pioneers facing food shortages sent a rescue party to another town for help. The group couldn't navigate its wagons through the deep snow, so its members ventured forth on foot, discovering that by laying their quilts down on the snow, they could walk without sinking. The event is commemorated at the town's annual Quilt Walk Festival.

Winter is prime time in Brian Head, one of Utah's highest-altitude ski resorts. Less crowded than bigger resorts to the north, it's known for its dry-powder skiing and, in warmer months, its mountain biking and hiking. Here, spas in mountain-view lodgings make it easy to soothe sore muscles or to simply relax amid clear mountain air.

With good restaurants, reliable lodging, and interesting museums, Cedar City is an ideal overnight stop between Bryce Canyon and Zion national parks. It was first called a "gateway to the parks" in the 1920s, when the park service and the railroad created iconic lodges for travelers eager to explore the region's natural wonders. Today, the community is further energized by students at Southern Utah University, which, in the 1960s, established the Utah Shakespeare Festival—another major draw throughout the summer.

Although the town of Tropic is tiny, it sits right outside Bryce Canyon National Park's eastern edge. Also east of Bryce is Escalante, the gateway to the Grand Staircase–Escalante National Monument, a wilderness area that is best explored with thoughtful planning and perhaps an experienced guide. Some exciting, scenic routes lace the area, too, including the evocatively named Hell's Backbone and Hole-in-the-Rock roads, where four-wheel-drive is recommended, and Highway 12 Scenic Byway.

Planning

Hotels

If you're looking for a spa experience and other resort-style amenities, hotels in Brian Head are your best bet. Cedar City has several inns, some with considerable historic charm. Elsewhere in the region, you'll find a mix of rustic lodges, B&Bs, and motels.

Restaurants

Hearty, down-to-earth fare is the norm in restaurants throughout the region. So is a laid-back, family-friendly vibe. Cedar City, a university town, offers a bit more variety, with a good assortment of ethnic restaurants. Note that some establishments don't serve alcohol and are closed on Sunday. A few also close seasonally.

Hotel and restaurant reviews have been shortened. For full information visit Fodors.com. Restaurant prices are the average cost of a main course at dinner, or if dinner is not served, at lunch. Hotel prices are the lowest cost of a standard double room in high season.

What It Costs			
$	$$	$$$	$$$$
RESTAURANTS			
under $16	$16–$22	$23–$30	over $30
HOTELS			
under $125	$125–$175	$176–$225	over $225

Along Scenic Highway 12, Red Canyon has several easy-to-access trails.

Panguitch

24 miles northwest of Bryce Canyon National Park.

An elevation of 6,650 feet helps this town of 1,700 residents keep its cool. Main Street is lined with late-19th-century buildings, and its early homes and outbuildings are noted for their distinctive brick architecture. Inexpensive lodging (mainly strip motels) and an excellent location 24 miles northwest of Bryce Canyon National Park and 31 miles east of Cedar Breaks National Monument make Panguitch a comfortable launching pad for recreation in the area.

GETTING HERE AND AROUND

Panguitch is along one of the region's prettiest main thoroughfares, U.S. 89, and is also near the starting point of scenic Highway 12, which leads to Bryce Canyon and Grand Staircase–Escalante.

ESSENTIALS

VISITOR INFORMATION Garfield County Office of Tourism.
☎ *800/444–6689, 435/676–1160* ⊕ *www.brycecanyoncountry. com.*

👁 Sights

★ Red Canyon

CANYON | Part of Dixie National Forest and easily accessed on the drive along Highway 12 from Panguitch to Bryce Canyon, this arresting 7,400-foot-elevation landscape of dark green Ponderosa pines and Douglas fir trees; fiery-red sandstone pinnacles and hoodoos; and clear blue sky makes for a memorable stop. Have a picnic and a short stroll on one of the several trails that lead from the Red Canyon Visitor Center (open late May to early September, Friday–Sunday). Longer treks—the Hoodoo Loop, Ledges, and Losee Canyon trails all showcase the rewarding scenery—are worth checking out if you have a bit more time. Some trails are well-suited to mountain biking, horseback riding, and cross-country skiing, and the paved 5-mile Red Canyon Trail is idea for road biking. There's also a campground. ⊠ *5375 Hwy. 12* ☎ *435/676–2676* ⊕ *www.fs.usda.gov/dixie.*

🍴 Restaurants

Burger Barn

$ | **BURGER** | **FAMILY** | Diners order at the window and sit at outdoor tables at this laid-back burger joint in a little red barn near Panguitch Lake, a great option en route between Bryce and Cedar Breaks National Monument or Cedar City. The one-third-pound Black Angus steak burgers here come with a variety of toppings, and the menu also has barbecue choices such as pulled pork or beef brisket sandwiches, fish-and-chips, sweet-potato fries, and shakes and ice cream. **Known for:** giant burgers and smoked meats; pretty setting near a mountain lake; ice cream sundaes. ⑤ *Average main: $9* ⊠ *75 S. Hwy. 143* ☎ *435/676–2445* ☉ *Closed mid-Sept.–mid-May.*

Cowboy's Smokehouse Café

$$ | **BARBECUE** | From the Western-style interior and creaky floors to the smoker out back, this rustic café has an aura of Texan authenticity—there are cowboy collectibles and game trophies lining the walls. No surprise that barbecue is the specialty here, with ample portions of favorites such as ribs, mesquite-flavored beef and pulled pork, and the restaurant's own house-made sauce, along with lighter sandwiches and salads. **Known for:** German sausage platter; prodigious steaks; delicious desserts, including fruit cobbler and pies. ⑤ *Average main: $21* ⊠ *95 N. Main St.* ☎ *435/676–8030* ⊕ *www.thecowboysmokehouse.com* ⊟ *No credit cards* ☉ *Closed Sun., closed late-Nov.–mid-Mar.*

Galaxy Diner & Motel

$ | **DINER** | **FAMILY** | This kitschy, '50s-style diner with a big chrome sign is popular with everyone from motorcyclists to families with young kids. Start the day with a hearty breakfast of sausage and gravy or eggs with elk; stop in later for a burger, sandwich, steak, or ribs—just save room for an old-time banana split or vanilla malt. **Known for:** fun retro decor; old-fashioned ice cream; big breakfast portions. $ *Average main: $13* ⌧ *216 N. Main St., Hatch* ☎ *435/735–4017* ⊕ *www.galaxyofhatch.com* ☻ *Closed Nov.–Mar.*

★ Tandoori Taqueria

$ | **FUSION** | The unfussy downtown eatery with indoor and outdoor tables has a novel concept, a fusion of Mexican and Indian cuisine, with creative tacos—braised pork with tomatillo chutney, slow-roasted beef and chorizo, and chicken tikka—leading the charge. There's also a veggie version with Bengali-style cauliflower and garbanzos mixed with Mexican spices, as well as tandoori chicken over rice. **Known for:** home-brewed kombuchas and chai teas; house-brined seasonal pickled veggies; honey-cardamom flan with a brûlée crust. $ *Average main: $12* ⌧ *5 N. Main St.* ☎ *435/962–9395* ⊕ *www.thetandooritaqueria.com* ☻ *No lunch Mon.–Thurs., closed Dec.–Apr.*

 ## Hotels

Church's Blue Pine Motel

$ | **HOTEL** | This single-story 1930s-era motel in Panguitch's cute historic district doesn't look like much from the outside, but the rooms are clean, have refrigerators and microwaves, and are among the most affordable within striking distance of Bryce, Zion, and Cedar Breaks. **Pros:** you can pull your car right up to your room; walking distance from local restaurants; rock-bottom rates. **Cons:** can be noisy; dated furnishings; not a lot to do right in Panguitch. $ *Rooms from: $79* ⌧ *130 N. Main St.* ☎ *435/676–8197, 800/299–6115* ⊕ *www.bluepinemotel.com* ⇲ *20 rooms* ⏹ *No meals.*

★ Cottonwood Meadow Lodge

$$$ | **RENTAL** | Set in a sweeping valley along the main road between Panguitch and Hatch, this sweet and secluded 50-acre ranch comprises four roomy cottages decorated with stylish Western-style furnishings—leather sofas, indigenous artwork, bearskin rugs, handcarved beds and tables—and outfitted with well-equipped kitchens. **Pros:** peaceful, scenic setting; convenient to Bryce and Zion; self-catering and large sitting areas make rooms nice for families. **Cons:** few dining options nearby; no a/c and no pets allowed; fills up well ahead on summer weekends.

⑤ *Rooms from: $185* ✉ *Mile Marker 123, U.S. 89* ☎ *435/676–8950* ⊕ *www.brycecanyoncabins.com* ⊃ *4 cabins* ⦿ *No meals.*

Mountain Ridge Cabins and Lodging
$ | HOTEL | In the tiny village of Hatch, 15 miles south of Panguitch, you'll find this nicely maintained and reasonably priced campus of cozy cabins and standard hotel rooms, all of them spotlessly clean and attractively decorated with modern furnishings, large flat-screen TVs, refrigerators, microwaves, and high-quality bedding. **Pros:** you can park right in front of your room; within walking distance of a few restaurants; convenient for exploring Bryce and Zion. **Cons:** least expensive rooms are quite small; in a tiny town; location off highway can be noisy. ⑤ *Rooms from: $109* ✉ *106 S. Main St., Hatch* ☎ *435/735–4300, 877/877–9939* ⊕ *www.moun-tainridgelodging.com* ⊘ *Closed Nov.–Apr.* ⊃ *24 rooms* ⦿ *No meals.*

Shopping

Bryce Canyon Trading Post
CRAFTS | Near Red Canyon a little east of where scenic Highway 12 begins at U.S. 89, this rambling emporium carries high-quality Native American turquoise jewelry, beadwork, textiles, and other fine crafts, plus a number of souvenirs related to the nearby national parks. ✉ *2938 Hwy. 12* ☎ *435/676–2688.*

Brian Head

36 miles southwest of Panguitch.

This tiny town's Brian Head Resort is Utah's southernmost and highest ski area at well over 9,000 feet, but the area's summer recreation, especially mountain biking, has also developed energetically in recent years. There are now more than 200 miles of trails for bikers, many of which are served by chairlift or shuttle services. The bright red-orange rock formations of Cedar Breaks National Monument are several miles south of town.

GETTING HERE AND AROUND
Most of the year, from Cedar City, you take Highway 14 east to highways 143 and 148 north. But in winter, when Highway 148 is closed, you'll need to take Interstate 15 north to Parowan and then Highway 143 south. Whichever way you arrive, the drive takes about the same amount of time (45 minutes to an hour) and is wonderfully scenic. If coming from Bryce Canyon, take Highway 12 west to U.S. 89; continue on it south through Hatch until you

Many visitors "explore" Cedar Breaks National Monument from roadside overlooks, so its trails are often blissfully crowd-free.

reach Highway 143 and continue west or take it north to Panguitch; and then take Highway 143 west from there. The distance is about the same.

Sights

★ Brian Head Peak Observation

SCENIC DRIVE | This 11,312-foot stone lookout hut was built by the Civilian Conservation Corps (CCC) in 1935 atop the highest summit in Iron County. You can see for miles in every direction, as far as Nevada and Arizona, enjoying especially dramatic views of nearby Cedar Breaks National Monument. The windy and dramatic nearly 3-mile drive along unpaved Forest Road 047 from Highway 143 is part of the fun; note that it's a short 0.2-mile hike from the parking area to the summit, and that when there's snow, the last section of road is closed to vehicles, but you can still hike or snowshoe up to the top. You can also hike to the summit from the junction of Rocky Road and Highway 143—the rugged and picturesque trek is about 3½ miles each way. ⊠ *End of Forest Rd. 047* ⊕ *www.fs.usda.gov/dixie.*

★ Cedar Breaks National Monument

NATIONAL/STATE PARK | From the rim of Cedar Breaks, a 3-mile-long natural amphitheater plunges a half-mile into the Markagunt Plateau. Short alpine hiking trails along the rim and few crowds make this a wonderful summer stop. Most visitors are content to photograph the monument from one of the handful of overlooks alongside the road—which means the intrepid hiker, skier, or snowshoer can easily find solitude along the trails. In fact, winter is one of the best times to visit, when snow drapes the red-or-ange formations. Call ahead for road conditions (the road is some-times closed due to heavy snowfall), and keep in mind that all visitor facilities are closed from October through late May. ⊠ *Hwy. 148 ✛ 3½ miles north of Hwy. 14* ☎ *435/586–9451* ⊕ *www.nps. gov/cebr* ✉ *$10 per person; free for ages 15 and under* ☉ *Visitor center closed mid-Oct.–late May.*

 Hotels

Best Western Premier Brian Head Hotel & Spa

$$ | **RESORT** | **FAMILY** | With its stunning scenery and prime loca-tion, this modern mission-style lodge is a great base for outdoor adventures and offers a number of amenities, including a bar and grill, outdoor deck, indoor pool, hot tubs, and a spa where you can enjoy a range of body and beauty treatments. **Pros:** com-fortable base for outdoor recreation; game room is popular with families; rooms have mountain views. **Cons:** can get pricey on winter weekends; breakfast costs extra; on-site restaurant gets mixed reviews. ⑤ *Rooms from: $145* ⊠ *314 Hunter Ridge Rd.* ☎ *435/677–9000* ⊕ *www.bwpbrianheadhotel.com* ➳ *112 rooms* ⦿ *No meals.*

Cedar Breaks Lodge

$$$ | **RESORT** | **FAMILY** | At an altitude of 9,600 feet, this lodge-style resort near Brian Head's popular ski slopes offers scenic views, and although some rooms may show their age, all are decorat-ed in a warm and rustic style that suits the setting. **Pros:** many recreational amenities; easy access to skiing, hiking, and mountain biking; scenic mountain views. **Cons:** early (10 am) check-out; no a/c; additional resort fee charged daily. ⑤ *Rooms from: $186* ⊠ *223 Hunter Ridge Rd.* ☎ *435/677–3000, 800/438–2929* ⊕ *www. cedarbreakslodge.com* ➳ *118 rooms* ⦿ *No meals.*

 Activities

BICYCLING

Brian Head is great for mountain biking excursions, offering a great variety of intriguing terrain, difficulty, and views. The area's most popular ride is the 12-mile Bunker Creek Trail, which winds through forests and meadows to Panguitch Lake. You don't have to bike up in elevation, as Brian Head Resort runs its ski lift in summer, giving access to several mountain-bike trails.

SKIING AND SNOWBOARDING

Brian Head Ski Resort

SKIING/SNOWBOARDING | Eight lifts (including two high-speed quads) transport skiers to this popular resort's 71 runs (evenly divided among expert, intermediate, and beginner terrain), which cover more than 650 acres and encompass a vertical drop of about 1,400 feet, with peak elevation nearing 11,000 feet. A half-pipe, trails, and a terrain park attract snowboarders. From the top of the resort's peak, you can see the red-rock cliffs of Cedar Breaks National Monument to the southwest. During summer and fall, the resort is a favorite with mountain bikers and hikers. ⊠ *329 S. Hwy. 143* ☎ *435/677–2035* ⊕ *www.brianhead.com* ✉ *Lift tickets $39–$83.*

Brianhead Sports

SKIING/SNOWBOARDING | As the largest outfitter in town, Brianhead Sports caters to cyclists, skiers, and snowboarders with equipment and accessories for rent or purchase. ⊠ *269 S. Village Way* ☎ *435/677–2014* ⊕ *www.brianheadsportsut.com.*

Georg's Ski Shop and Bikes

BICYCLING | Just down the road from Brian Head Resort, this popular ski shop has new and rental skis, snowboards, and bikes. The friendly staff is experienced at helping both beginning and advanced skiers find the perfect gear. ⊠ *612 S. Hwy. 143* ☎ *435/677–2013* ⊕ *www.georgsskishop.com.*

Cedar City

33 miles west of Brian Head.

Rich iron-ore deposits captured the attention of Mormon leader Brigham Young. He ordered a Church of Jesus Christ of Latter-day Saints mission be established here in what is now southwestern Utah's second largest community, with a population of about 35,000 (up from just 13,000 in 1990). The first ironworks and foundry opened in 1851 and operated for only eight years; problems with the furnace, flooding, and hostility between settlers and regional Native Americans eventually put out the flame. Residents then turned to ranching and farming for their livelihood, and Cedar City has thrived as an agricultural center ever since.

Since the founding of Southern Utah University in 1897, the city has been an educational and cultural hub as well. The university campus hosts the community's most popular event: the Utah Shakespeare Festival, whose season runs from late June through October. This attractive, youthful gateway to both Zion and Bryce

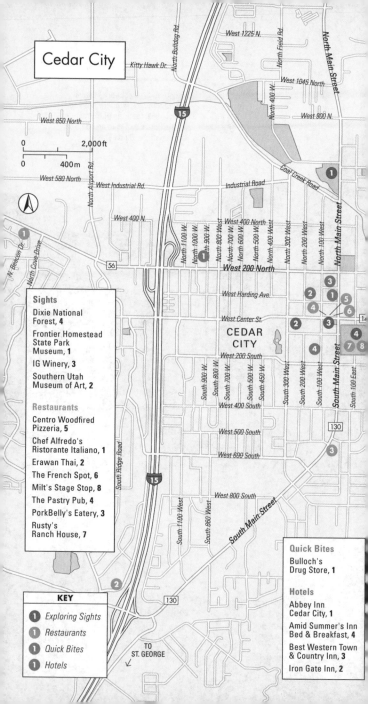

Cedar City

West 1225 N.
Kitty Hawk Dr.
North Buildog Rd.
North Field Rd.
North Main Street
West 1045 North
West 400 W.
I-15
West 900 N.
West 850 North
0   2,000 ft
0   400 m
Coal Creek Road
West 580 North
West Industrial Rd.
North Airport Rd.
Industrial Road
West 400 N.
N. Beacon Dr.
North Cove Drive
West 400 North
North 1100 W.
North 1000 W.
North 900 W.
North 800 West
North 700 West
North 600 West
North 500 West
North 400 West
North 300 West
North 200 West
North 100 West
North Main Street
56
West 200 North
West Harding Ave.

Sights

Dixie National
Forest, **4**

Frontier Homestead
State Park
Museum, **1**

IG Winery, **3**

Southern Utah
Museum of Art, **2**

Restaurants

Centro Woodfired
Pizzeria, **5**

Chef Alfredo's
Ristorante Italiano, **1**

Erawan Thai, **2**

The French Spot, **6**

Milt's Stage Stop, **8**

The Pastry Pub, **4**

PorkBelly's Eatery, **3**

Rusty's
Ranch House, **7**

West Center St.
CEDAR
CITY
West 200 South
West 400 South
South 900 W.
South 800 W.
South 700 W.
South 600 W.
South 500 W.
South 450 W.
South 300 West
South 200 West
South 100 West
South Main Street
South 100 East
West 500 South
130
West 600 South
South Ridge Road
The French Spot, 6
I-15
West 800 South
South 1100 West
South 860 West
South Main Street
130
TO
ST. GEORGE

KEY

1	*Exploring Sights*
1	*Restaurants*
1	*Quick Bites*
1	*Hotels*

Quick Bites

Bulloch's
Drug Store, **1**

Hotels

Abbey Inn
Cedar City, **1**

Amid Summer's Inn
Bed & Breakfast, **4**

Best Western Town
& Country Inn, **3**

Iron Gate Inn, **2**

Canyon national parks is also well situated for exploring the Brian Head area and Cedar Breaks National Monument.

GETTING HERE AND AROUND

Interstate 15 cuts right through Cedar City. Though downtown is walkable, you'll want a car to explore further afield.

FESTIVALS

★ Utah Shakespeare Festival

FESTIVALS | Since 1962, Cedar City has gone Bard-crazy, staging productions of Shakespeare's plays from the end of June through late October in three Southern Utah University campus theaters, the largest of which is an open-air replica of Shakespeare's Globe Theatre. The Tony award–winning festival also features literary seminars, backstage tours, cabarets showcasing festival actors, and an outdoor pre-show with Elizabethan performers. Try to book well in advance, as many performances sell out. ☎ 435/586–7878, 800/752–9849 ⊕ www.bard.org.

ESSENTIALS

VISITOR INFORMATION Visit Cedar City and Brian Head. ⊠ 581 N. Main St. ☎ 435/586–5124 ⊕ www.visitcedarcity.com.

 Sights

Dixie National Forest

FOREST | The forest's expansive natural area is divided into four noncontiguous swaths covering a total of nearly 2 million acres. Adjacent to three national parks, two national monuments, and several state parks, the forest has 26 campgrounds with a variety of backdrops, including lakes, mountains, and pine and spruce forests. Hiking, picnicking, horseback riding, and fishing are among the recreational opportunities here. ⊠ Cedar City ☎ 435/865–3700 ⊕ www.fs.usda.gov/dixie.

Frontier Homestead State Park Museum

MUSEUM | **FAMILY** | This interactive living-history museum devoted to the county's early iron industry is home to a number of interesting attractions, including a bullet-scarred stagecoach that ran in the days of Butch Cassidy and the oldest standing home in all of southern Utah, built in 1851. Local artisans demonstrate pioneer crafts, and numerous mining artifacts and tools are on display. ⊠ 585 N. Main St. ☎ 435/586–9290 ⊕ www.frontierhomestead. org ☑ $4 ☉ Closed Sun. in Sept.–May.

IG Winery

WINERY/DISTILLERY | In a state with few wineries, this popular operation in downtown Cedar City sources grapes from respected vineyards in California's Napa and Sonoma Valleys, Washington's Columbia Valley, and Oregon's Rogue Valley. The Bordeaux-style reds are well-crafted, though spendy, while more moderately priced Tempranillo and Sangiovese also have plenty of fans. With exposed brick walls and hardwood floors, the handsome tasting room is hung with local art and warmed by a fireplace in winter. There's also a sunny patio, and live bands perform regularly. ⊠ *59 W. Center St.* ☎ *435/867–9463* ⊕ *www.igwinery.com* ☉ *Closed Sun. and Mon.*

Southern Utah Museum of Art

MUSEUM | Set in a striking modern building designed in 2016 to resemble the region's canyons and rock formations, this excellent regional art museum with a peaceful sculpture garden is part of Southern Utah University's cultural compound, along with the Utah Shakespeare Festival theaters. The galleries feature selections from the museum's permanent collection of some 2,000 works—including pieces by Renoir, Dalí, and Thomas Hart Benton—along with rotating shows that shine a light on emerging regional artists as well as students and faculty. ⊠ *13 S. 300 W* ☎ *435/586–5432* ⊕ *www.suu.edu/pva/suma* ☉ *Closed Sun.*

🍴 Restaurants

★ Centro Woodfired Pizzeria

$ | PIZZA | You can watch your handmade artisanal pizza being pulled from the fires of the brick oven, then sit back and enjoy a seasonal pie layered with ingredients like house-made fennel sausage and wood-roasted cremini mushrooms. The creamy vanilla gelato layered with a balsamic reduction and sea salt is highly addictive. **Known for:** house-made sausage; good wine and beer list; creative desserts. ⑤ *Average main: $14* ⊠ *50 W. Center St.* ☎ *435/867–8123* ⊕ *www.centropizzeria.com.*

Chef Alfredo's Ristorante Italiano

$$ | ITALIAN | With linen tablecloths, a decent wine list, soft background music, and authentic Sicilian-style food, this restaurant tucked away in a strip mall is charmingly old-school. Highlights include fresh-baked bread served with olive oil; traditional antipasto appetizers; specials like butternut ravioli or eggplant Parmesan; and entrees such as linguine in clam sauce or fettuccine primavera, as well as six chicken-breast options—from parmigiana to marsala. **Known for:** romantic atmosphere; flatbread pizzas; tender steaks. [$] *Average main: $22* ✉ *2313 W. 400 N* ☎ *435/586–2693* ⊕ *www.chefalfredos.com* ⊗ *No lunch Fri.–Sun.*

Erawan Thai

$$ | THAI | In a nondescript but conveniently located shopping center just off the interstate, this excellent Thai restaurant has a cheerful, inviting, rustic-wood interior with paintings, crafts, and cannisters of imported tea. The kitchen turns out deftly prepared renditions of classic dishes—chicken satay, tom kha soup—as well as such creative fare as mango-curry fried rice, barbecue chicken in Thai spices, and five different entrees featuring elk. **Known for:** attractive, art-filled space; crispy duck with several preparations; extensive selection of teas. [$] *Average main: $17* ✉ *1190 Sage Dr.* ☎ *435/267–0391* ⊕ *www.erawanthai-ut.com* ⊗ *Closed Sun.*

★ The French Spot

$$ | FRENCH | This tiny takeout patisserie in the center of downtown is a favorite stop for lattes and cold brew; crepes and salads; heartier dinner specials (salmon, filet mignon); and ethereal pastries and sweets, including a rotating selection of chocolate, berry, lemon, and seasonal tarts. Although primarily a to-go option that's perfect for stocking up before a hiking or biking adventure, in warm weather, you can also dine on the cute patio out front. **Known for:** picnic supplies to enjoy before a show at the nearby Utah Shakespeare Festival; scrambled-egg breakfast croissants with ham, bacon, Gruyère, or smoked salmon; colorful macarons. [$] *Average main: $17* ✉ *5 N. Main St.* ☎ *347/886–8587* ⊕ *www. thefrenchspotcafe.com.*

Milt's Stage Stop

$$$ | STEAKHOUSE | Cabin decor, friendly service, and canyon views are the hallmarks of this dinner spot 10 minutes southeast of downtown Cedar City by car. Expect traditional, hearty steak house cuisine: rib-eye steaks, prime rib, and seafood dishes, accompanied by loaded baked potatoes, deep-fried zucchini, and similar sides. **Known for:** scenic alpine setting; hefty steaks and seafood; apple crisp a la mode. [$] *Average main: $27* ✉ *3560 E. Hwy. 14* ☎ *435/586–9344* ⊕ *www.miltsstagestop.com* ⊗ *No lunch.*

The Pastry Pub

$ | CAFÉ | FAMILY | Don't be fooled by the name—coffee and tea are the only brews here, but pastries aren't the only thing on the menu. Build a sandwich of meat, egg, cheese, and more on a freshly baked bagel, croissant, artisan bread, or one of four flavors of wraps. **Known for:** walk from the Shakespeare Festival;

espresso; seasonal soups. $ *Average main: $10* ⊠ *86 W. Center St.* ☎ *435/867–1400* ⊕ *www.cedarcitypastrypub.com* ✆ *Closed Sun.*

PorkBelly's Eatery

$ | **AMERICAN** | As the name suggests, this airy contemporary restaurant is a meat-lover's paradise. Starting with tri-tip eggs Benedict and chicken and waffles at breakfast, pulled-pork sandwiches, carne asada nachos, and bacon-mushroom-cheddar burgers follow. **Known for:** mammoth portions of meat-centric fare; smoked baby back ribs on weekends; the chicken bomb (a jalapeño stuffed with cream cheese and sausage and wrapped in chicken and bacon). $ *Average main: $14* ⊠ *565 S. Main St.* ☎ *435/586–5285* ⊕ *www.porkbellyseatery.com* ✆ *Closed Mon. No dinner Sun.*

Rusty's Ranch House

$$$ | **STEAKHOUSE** | Locals have long considered the meals at this fun, if a bit touristy, Old West–style roadhouse some of the best in the region. They serve steaks, barbecue brisket and baby back ribs, towering burgers, sweet coconut shrimp, and other classics. **Known for:** extensive cocktail selection; quirky Western vibe; Granny's hot-caramel apple cobbler. $ *Average main: $25* ⊠ *2275 E. Hwy. 14* ☎ *435/586–3839* ⊕ *www.rustysranchhouse.com* ✆ *Closed Sun. No lunch.*

☕ Coffee and Quick Bites

Bulloch's Drug Store

$ | **CAFÉ** | **FAMILY** | Built in 1917 and remodeled to retain its historic character, this landmark building in downtown Cedar City contains an old-fashioned drug store, complete with a soda fountain from the 1950s. Enjoy ice cream, shakes, sundaes, and malts, or try one of the uniquely flavored sodas. **Known for:** decadent ice cream sundaes; big selection of penny candies; cool old building. $ *Average main: $5* ⊠ *91 N. Main St.* ☎ *435/586–9651* ⊕ *www. bullochdrug.com* ✆ *Closed Sun. No dinner.*

🛏 Hotels

Abbey Inn Cedar City

$ | **HOTEL** | Just off the interstate and near Southern Utah University, this two-story economical motel has spacious rooms with exterior entrances, fridges, microwaves, and—in the case of suites—kitchens and jetted tubs. **Pros:** 10-minute walk to downtown and festival venues; lots of dining options nearby; nice indoor pool and fitness center. **Cons:** road noise for some rooms; bland setting amid fast-food restaurants and chains; cookie-cutter room decor.

⑤ *Rooms from: $126* ✉ *940 W. 200 N* ☎ *435/586–9966, 800/325–5411* ⊕ *www.abbeyinncedar.com* ⤴ *83 rooms* ⧓ *Free breakfast.*

★ Amid Summer's Inn Bed & Breakfast
$ | **B&B/INN** | This enchanting 1930s cottage-style inn, set along a quiet tree-lined street close to the Southern Utah University campus, has individually decorated rooms with literary themes, lavish antiques, and fine artwork. **Pros:** friendly, knowledgeable staff; exceptional breakfasts and decadent baked goods; two blocks from Shakespeare Festival and downtown. **Cons:** some rooms are accessible only by a narrow stairway; may be too intimate for some; books up well in advance in summer. ⑤ *Rooms from: $119* ✉ *140 S. 100 W* ☎ *435/586–2600* ⊕ *www.amidsummersinn.com* ⤴ *10 rooms* ⧓ *Free breakfast.*

Best Western Town & Country Inn
$ | **HOTEL** | **FAMILY** | In downtown Cedar City, this renovated motel offers spacious rooms, complimentary breakfast, a fitness center, pool, and two on-site eateries. **Pros:** easy to walk to shops and restaurants; great on-site pool; comfortable beds and pillows. **Cons:** breakfast gets mixed reviews; older property; rooms open to outside. ⑤ *Rooms from: $113* ✉ *189 N. Main St.* ☎ *435/586–9900* ⊕ *www.bestwestern.com* ⤴ *145 rooms* ⧓ *Free Breakfast.*

★ Iron Gate Inn
$$ | **B&B/INN** | Set in a grand downtown second-empire Victorian home that underwent an ambitious renovation before becoming a B&B, this gracious lodging has seven large, period-furnished rooms with well-designed modern bathrooms; some have private sitting areas or direct access to verandas and the inn's fragrant gardens. **Pros:** steps from Shakespeare Festival and downtown; impressive gourmet breakfast included; Jacuzzi and firepit in lush back garden. **Cons:** frilly Victorian decor may not suit every taste; friendly cats and dogs live on premises but could be an issue for some; fills up on summer weekends. ⑤ *Rooms from: $149* ✉ *100 N. 200 W* ☎ *435/383–5133* ⊕ *www.theirongateinn.com* ⤴ *7 rooms* ⧓ *Free breakfast.*

Activities

RECREATIONAL AREAS
Coal Creek Trail
PARK—SPORTS-OUTDOORS | **FAMILY** | It's easy, even if you're pushing a stroller, to get out into nature in this sunny, mile-high community. Perfect for strolling, jogging, biking, or running, this 3.4-mile paved multipurpose trail starts in Bicentennial Park and cuts in a southeasterly direction right through the center of town, paralleling the

scenic creek for which it's named and eventually joining with the similarly paved Cedar Canyon Trail. Other non-paved hiking trails also spur off from the Cedar Creek Trail and into the surrounding foothills. ⊠ *Bicentennial Park, 660 W. 1045 N* ⊕ *www.cedarcity. org.*

Tropic

28 miles east of Panguitch.

Essentially an extension of nearby Bryce Canyon City and thus a similar base for exploring the majestic rock formations of Bryce Canyon National Park—many of which you can see from town—Tropic has around 500 residents and a handful of eateries and lodgings, some of them excellent. Keep in mind that many businesses shut down or greatly slow down in winter.

GETTING HERE AND AROUND
Just down the hill from Bryce Canyon, tiny Tropic is along Highway 12.

 Restaurants

★ Stone Hearth Grille
$$$$ | **MODERN AMERICAN** | With sweeping panoramas toward Bryce Canyon from the back deck, an art-filled dining room with a stone fireplace, and some of the most accomplished modern American fare within an hour's drive of the park, this refined yet unpretentious restaurant on the outskirts of tiny Tropic is well worth a splurge. Favorites here include grilled artichoke with hollandaise sauce, radicchio Caesar salad, bone-in grilled pork chops with cheddar-potato fondue, and several preparations of local grass-fed steaks. **Known for:** breathtaking views; well-curated wine list; great children's menu. ⑤ *Average main: $31* ⊠ *1380 W. Stone Canyon La., Tropic* ☎ *435/679–8923* ⊕ *www.stonehearthgrille.com* ☉ *Closed Nov.–mid-Mar.*

 Hotels

★ Stone Canyon Inn
$$$ | **B&B/INN** | Although not actually in the park, this stunningly situated luxury inn lies just east of Bryce Canyon, and rooms and the excellent on-site restaurant, Stone Hearth Grille, have astounding views of the park's hoodoos—there's even a trailhead nearby that accesses some of Bryce's best trails. **Pros:** the most

A surreal canyon in Grand Staircase–Escalante, a national monument administered by the Bureau of Land Management.

stylish rooms in the area; fantastic restaurant on-site; soaking tubs and fireplaces in some rooms. **Cons:** on the pricey side; not within walking distance of downtown shops and restaurants; no breakfast. ⑤ *Rooms from: $195* ✉ *1380 W. Stone Canyon La., Tropic* ☎ *435/679–8611, 866/489–4680* ⊕ *www.stonecanyoninn. com* 🛏 *15 rooms* ⑩ *No meals*.

Escalante

39 miles northeast of Tropic.

Though the Dominguez and Escalante expedition of 1776 came nowhere near this area, the town's name does honor the Spanish explorer. It was bestowed nearly a century later by a member of a survey party led by John Wesley Powell, charged with mapping this remote area. Today, this friendly little town is home to a steadily growing crop of lodgings, eateries, and tour operators. Escalante is the northern gateway to Grand Staircase–Escalante National Monument, an amazing wilderness that earned monument status in September 1996 when 1.9 million acres were set aside. In 2017, however, nearly 1 million acres were removed from protection by presidential proclamation. Conservation and environmental organizations sued to overturn that change, stating that the president's actions were unlawful. The lawsuit had not yet been ruled on at the time of this writing.

Unlike parks and monuments operated by the National Park Service, Grand Staircase–Escalante is administered by the Bureau of Land Management (BLM), and visiting its key attractions requires a bit more research and effort than, for example, Bryce Canyon, which is relatively more compact and accessible. A good way to plan your visit is to stop by one of the several visitor centers, such as the Escalante Interagency office right in town or the BLM Visitor Center in Cannonville.Given that many of this national monument's top attractions are in remote areas with limited signage and accessed via unpaved roads, it may be worth hiring one of the experienced outfitters and guides in the area, especially if it's your first visit. The monument's top attractions include Calf Creek Falls and the several sites on or just off of Hole-in-the-Rock Road.

GETTING HERE AND AROUND

Escalante is accessible by Highway 12, one of the prettiest drives in the state, especially the stretch that runs north to Boulder. You can explore the vast Grand Staircase–Escalante National Monument via unpaved roads (some of which are pretty rough), ideally with a four-wheel-drive vehicle, although in dry weather, a passenger car can handle some areas. Most access points are off of Highway 12. It costs nothing to enter the park, but fees apply for camping and backcountry permits.

ESSENTIALS

VISITOR INFORMATION Cannonville BLM Visitor Center. ✉ *10 Center St., Cannonville* ☎ *435/826–5640* ⊕ *www.blm.gov/visit/ cannonville-visitor-center.* **Escalante Interagency Visitor Center.** ✉ *755 W. Main St.* ☎ *435/826–5499* ⊕ *www.blm.gov/visit/ escalante-interagency-visitor-center.*

TOURS

Escalante Outfitters

SPECIAL-INTEREST | Guided fly-fishing excursions as well as natural history tours of Grand Staircase–Escalante National Monument and Boulder Mountain are offered here. The business also has an outfitter store with camping gear, café, small sleeping cabins, and campsites. ✉ *310 W. Main St.* ☎ *435/826–4266* ⊕ *www.escalante-outfitters.com* 🍴 *From $45.*

Escape Goats

SPECIAL-INTEREST | This noted family-owned operation offers a variety of day and evening hikes, multiday backpacking trips, and photo and artist tours, which can be customized to any ability or age. The company provides shuttle services, too. ✉ *Escalante* ☎ *435/826–4652* ⊕ *www.escalantecanyonguides.com* 🍴 *From $150.*

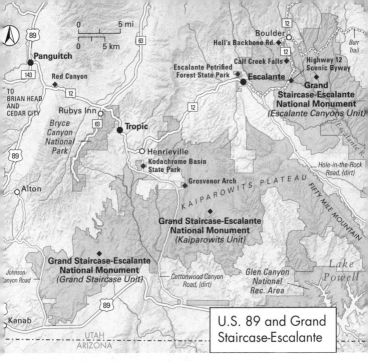

U.S. 89 and Grand
Staircase-Escalante

Excursions of Escalante

ADVENTURE TOURS | Hiking, backpacking, photography, and can-
yoneering tours in the Escalante region are custom-fit to your
needs and abilities by experienced guides. Canyoneers will be
taken into the slot canyons to move through slot chutes or rappel
down walls and other obstacles. All gear and provisions are pro-
vided whether it's a day hike or multiday adventure. ⊠ *125 E. Main
St.* ☎ *800/839–7567, 435/826–4714* ⊕ *www.excursionsofescalan-
te.com* ⊠ *From $165.*

★ Utah Canyon Outdoors

SPECIAL-INTEREST | Run by a young husband and wife team with
extensive experience in Utah as naturalists and guides, this
stellar outfitter operates an outdoor gear shop and coffeehouse
in a charming little converted house in downtown Escalante.
In addition to full-day hikes through slot canyons and the area's
other dramatic features, the company also offers Escalante yoga
experiences. ⊠ *325 W. Main St.* ☎ *435/826–4967* ⊕ *www.utah-
canyonoutdoors.com* ⊠ *From $140.*

Did You Know?

Reaching Grand Staircase–
Escalante's cathedral-like,
150-foot-wide, 100-foot-high
Jacob Hamblin Arch in Coyote
Gulch is an adventure, involving a
bumpy, dusty drive and a lengthy,
strenuous hike.

Sights

★ Calf Creek Falls Recreation Area

NATIONAL/STATE PARK | FAMILY | One of the more easily accessible and rewarding adventures in the area, this picturesque canyon rife with oak trees and cacti and sandstone pictographs is reached via a 6-mile round-trip hike that starts at Calf Creek Campground, which is just 15 miles east of Escalante and 12 miles south of Boulder along scenic Highway 12. The big payoff, and it's especially pleasing on warm days, is a 126-foot spring-fed waterfall. The pool at the base is a beautiful spot for a swim or picnic. ⊠ *Hwy. 12* ☎ *435/826–5499* ⊕ *www.blm.gov/visit/calf-creek-recreation-area-day-use-site* ⊡ *$5 per vehicle.*

Escalante Petrified Forest State Park

NATIONAL/STATE PARK | FAMILY | This park just 2 miles outside Escalante protects a huge repository of petrified wood, easily spotted along two short but moderately taxing hiking trails (the shorter and steeper of the two, the Sleeping Rainbows Trail, requires some scrambling over boulders). Of equal interest is the park's Wide Hollow Reservoir, which has a swimming beach and is popular for kayaking, standup paddling, trout fishing, and birding. ⊠ *710 N. Reservoir Rd.* ☎ *435/826–4466* ⊕ *stateparks.utah. gov/parks/escalante-petrified-forest/* ⊡ *$8 per vehicle.*

★ Hell's Backbone Road

SCENIC DRIVE | For a scenic, topsy-turvy backcountry drive or a challenging mountain-bike ride, follow 35-mile Hell's Backbone Road (aka Forest Road 153) from Escalante, where it begins as Posey Lake Road, to Boulder. Built by the Civilian Conservation Corps in the early 1930s, it's a gravel-surface alternate route that's arguably even more spectacular than scenic Highway 12. You can make the drive with an ordinary passenger car in summer (it's impassable in winter), assuming dry conditions, but a four-wheel-drive vehicle is more comfortable. Allow about two hours to drive it. ⊠ *Hell's Backbone Rd.*

★ Highway 12 Scenic Byway

SCENIC DRIVE | Keep your camera handy and steering wheel steady along this entrancing 123-mile route between Escalante and Torrey, just west of Capitol Reef National Park. Though the highway starts at the intersection of U.S. 89, west of Bryce Canyon National Park, the stretch that begins in Escalante is one of the most spectacular. Be sure to stop at the scenic overlooks; almost every one will give you an eye-popping view, and information panels let you know what you're looking at. Pay attention while driving, though; the paved road is twisting and steep, and at times climbs over a hogback with sheer drop-offs on both sides. ⊠ *Hwy. 12*.

Hole-in-the-Rock Road

SCENIC DRIVE | On the way to southeastern Utah in 1879, Mormon pioneers chipped and blasted a narrow passageway in solid rock, through which they lowered their wagons. The Hole-in-the-Rock Trail, now a very rugged 60-mile unpaved washboard road (aka BLM 200), leads south from Highway 12, 5 miles east of Escalante, to the actual hole-in-the-rock site in Glen Canyon Recreation Area. The original passageway ends where the canyon has been flooded by the waters of Lake Powell—you can hike the half-mile from the end of the road to a dramatic viewpoint overlooking the lake. Just keep in mind that it can take up to three hours to drive to the end of the road, and high-clearance vehicles are best (and a requirement when muddy—check with the Escalante BLM visitor center before setting out). However, there are some amazing hiking spots located off the road, including Zebra Slot Canyon (at mile 8.5), Devil's Garden (at mile 12), Peekaboo Gulch (off Dry Fork Road, at mile 26), and Dance Hall Rock (at mile 36). ⊠ *Hole-in-the-Rock Road* ☎ *435/826–5499* ⊕ *www.nps.gov/glca/learn/historyculture/holeintherock.htm*.

★ Kodachrome Basin State Park

NATIONAL/STATE PARK | FAMILY | Yes, it is named after the old-fashioned color photo film, and once you see it you'll understand why the National Geographic Society gave it the name. The stone spires known as "sand pipes" cannot be found anywhere else in the world. Hike any of the trails to spot some of the 67 pipes in and around the park. The short Angels Palace Trail takes you quickly into the park's interior, up, over, and around some of the badlands. Note that the oft-photographed Shakespeare Arch collapsed in April 2019, although the trail leading to it is still open. ⊠ *Off Cottonwood Canyon Rd., Cannonville* ☎ *435/679–8562* ⊕ *stateparks.utah.gov/parks/kodachrome-basin/* ⚐ *$10 per vehicle*.

🍽 Restaurants

★ Escalante Outfitters Restaurant

$ | MODERN AMERICAN | This warm and inviting log cabin–style restaurant—operated by a popular tour operator that also runs a camp store and cabin and camping compound—is a great place to sit back and relax after a day of hiking, fly-fishing, or road-tripping. Try one of the creatively topped pizzas, a veggie sandwich, or an apple-pecan-arugula salad, or drop in for one of the best

The National Geographic Society gave colorful Kodachrome Basin State Park its very apt name.

cups of (Fair Trade) coffee in the region and a light breakfast to kick off the day. **Known for:** one of the better craft beer selections in the region; lively and fun dining room; fine coffees, quiches, and pastries in the morning. $ *Average main: $12* ⊠ *310 W. Main St.* ☎ *435/826–4266* ⊕ *www.escalanteoutfitters.com* ⊗ *Closed Dec.–Feb.*

☕ Coffee and Quick Bites

★ Kiva Koffeehouse

$ | CAFÉ | This fun stop along scenic Highway 12 at mile marker 73.86, 13 miles east of Escalante, was constructed by the late artist and inventor Bradshaw Bowman, who began building it when he was in his eighties and spent two years finding and transporting the 13 Douglas-fir logs surrounding the structure. The distinctive eatery with amazing views serves homemade soups, bagel sandwiches, salads, and desserts, and an array of espresso drinks. **Known for:** breathtaking canyon views; breakfast sandwiches and bagels; housemade pies and cupcakes. $ *Average main: $10* ⊠ *Escalante* ✛ *Hwy. 12 between mileposts 73 and 74* ☎ *435/826–4550* ⊕ *www.kivakoffeehouse.com* ⊟ *No credit cards* ⊗ *Closed Nov.–Feb. and Mon.–Tues. No dinner.*

Hotels

Canyon Country Lodge

$$$ | **HOTEL** | **FAMILY** | A boutique hotel on the outskirts of town, just off Highway 12, Canyon Country Lodge contains 28 spacious rooms—many of them with northerly views toward Escalante Canyon—comfortably outfitted with smart TVs, microwaves, refrigerators, and modern tile bathrooms. **Pros:** stylishly decorated; nice indoor pool and hot tub; close to but just outside downtown. **Cons:** 15-minute walk to most dining options; on-site restaurant gets mixed reviews; no elevator. $ *Rooms from: $199* ✉ *760 E. Hwy. 12* ☎ *435/826–4545, 844/367–3080* ⊕ *www.canyoncountrylodge.com* ⟲ *28 rooms* ⟨◯⟩ *Free breakfast.*

Circle D Motel

$ | **HOTEL** | Although there's nothing fancy about this low-slung adobe motel on the edge of downtown Escalante, the simple rooms have all the basics you need for a comfortable night or two—microwaves, fridges, coffeemakers, HDTVs, climate control—and one larger suite with a kitchenette sleeps six. **Pros:** short walk from downtown businesses; casual restaurant with a pleasant patio; among the lowest rates in the area. **Cons:** standard rooms are small; no pool or gym; no breakfast. $ *Rooms from: $86* ✉ *475 W. Main St.* ☎ *435/826–4297* ⊕ *www.escalantecircledmotel.com* ⟲ *22 rooms* ⟨◯⟩ *No meals.*

★ Entrada Escalante Lodge

$$ | **HOTEL** | Each of the eight rooms in this smart, contemporary lodge in Escalante has a patio with grand views of the surrounding mountains, plus plenty of cushy perks like French presses and fresh-ground coffee, plush bedding, and 50-inch smart TVs. **Pros:** stunning views of Grand Staircase–Escalante National Monument; spacious rooms; pets are welcome in some rooms and the property is horse friendly, too. **Cons:** books up well ahead many weekends; in a very secluded, small town; no gym or pool. $ *Rooms from: $139* ✉ *480 W. Main St.* ☎ *435/826–4000* ⊕ *www.entradaescalante.com* ✹ *Closed Jan.–Feb.* ⟲ *8 rooms* ⟨◯⟩ *No meals.*

Escalante Outfitters Cabins

$ | **B&B/INN** | If you don't care about frills but do plan on adventuring in the area, consider one of this property's seven log, bunkhouse cabins, which share a bathhouse, or the large family cabin that sleeps four and has its own bathroom; tent sites are also available. **Pros:** fire pit, grills, and picnic tables; pet-friendly; hotel is also an outfitter/operator offering lots of tours. **Cons:**

cabins are tiny; you may have to wait in line for a shower; some cabins have only bunk beds. $ *Rooms from: $55* ✉ *310 W. Main St.* ☎ *435/826–4266* ⊕ *www.escalanteoutfitters.com* ⊗ *Closed Dec.–Feb.* 🛏 *8 cabins* ﹖⊙﹖ *No meals.*

★ Slot Canyons Inn B&B

$$ | **B&B/INN** | Set in a dramatic, New Mexico adobe–style building, this upscale inn with spacious rooms and lots of big windows is 5 miles west of town—at the mouth of a canyon on the edge of the national monument—and has hikes right outside its door, as well as hosts who can provide guidance on regional treks. **Pros:** utterly peaceful and enchanting setting; within a short hike of petroglyphs and dramatic cliffs; many rooms have jetted soaking tubs. **Cons:** very remote setting; the one economically priced room is a little small; not within walking distance of town. $ *Rooms from: $125* ✉ *3680 Hwy. 12* ☎ *435/826–4901* ⊕ *www.slotcanyonsinn. com* 🛏 *11 rooms* ﹖⊙﹖ *Free breakfast.*

Nightlife

★ 4th West Pub

BARS/PUBS | In a part of the world where nightlife typically consists of listening to coyotes howl beneath a starlit sky, it's nice to have one good late-night ("late" meaning 10 or 11 pm, depending on the season) option. Set in a stylishly converted, circa-1940s service station, this is a great place to socialize, shoot pool, and sip craft beer and cocktails. There's live music, art classes, trivia matches, and other fun events on some evenings, and the kitchen turns out tasty bar snacks, from nachos to panini. Note that the pub is closed Sunday and Monday during the winter. ✉ *425 W. Main St.* ☎ *435/826–4525* ⊕ *www.4wpub.com.*

Shopping

Serenidad Gallery

ART GALLERIES | This gallery and shop features watercolors of local scenes by owner Harriet Priska, along with antiques, Native American jewelry and pottery, petrified wood, rocks, and other crafts and gift items. ✉ *170 S. 100 West* ☎ *435/826–4720* ⊕ *www. facebook.com/serenidadgalleryescalanteutah* ⊗ *Closed Sun.*

Index

A

Abbey Inn Cedar City 🖼 , *172–173*
Accessibility concerns, *34*
Admission fees, *34, 57, 123*
Advenire, The 🖼 , *110*
Adventure tours, *25, 81, 125*
Agua Canyon, *141*
Air tours, *148*
Air travel, *30, 47, 54*
Airports, *27, 30, 47*
Amid Summer's Inn Bed & Breakfast 🖼 , *173*
Angel's Landing Trail, *20, 64–65*
Antelopes, *17*
Aragosta ✕ , *107*

B

Benja Thai and Sushi ✕ , *107*
Best Western Bryce Canyon Grand Hotel 🖼 , *146*
Best Western Coral Hills 🖼 , *110*
Best Western East Zion Thunderbird Lodge 🖼 , *114*
Best Western Plus Ruby's Inn 🖼 , *146*
Best Western Premier Brian Head Hotel & Spa 🖼 , *165*
Bicycles Unlimited, *112–113*
Bicycling
Brian Head, *165*
Bryce Canyon, *148–149*
Hurricane, *101*
St, George, *112–113*
Zion, *82*
Bighorn sheep, *16*
Bike Zion, *82*
Birds, *16, 17*
Bird-watching
Bryce Canyon, *149*
Zion, *82–83*
Bit & Spur Restaurant and Saloon ✕ , *96*
Books and movies about, *26*
Brian Head, *157, 163–166*
Brian Head Peak Observation, *164*
Brian Head Ski Resort, *166*
Brigham Young Winter Home, *102*
Bristlecone Loop Trail, *143–144*
Bryce Amphitheater, *116, 125*
Bryce Canyon Airlines & Helicopters, *148*
Bryce Canyon Astronomy Fest, *45*
Bryce Canyon City, *116, 144–146, 148*
Bryce Canyon Country Rodeo, *44*
Bryce Canyon Gateways, *14, 156–184*
Brian Head, *157, 163–166*
Cedar City, *157, 166, 169–174*
dining, *159, 161–162, 170–172, 174, 181–182*
Escalante, *157, 175–177*
festivals, *157*
lodging, *159, 162–163, 165, 172–173, 174–175, 183–184*
nightlife, *184*
Panguitch, *156, 160–163*
price categories, *159*
shopping, *163, 184*
sports and activities, *165–166, 173–174*
top reasons to go, *156*
Tropic, *157, 174–175*
visitor centers, *176*
visitor information, *160, 169, 176*
Bryce Canyon General Store, *140*
Bryce Canyon Geology Fest, *45*
Bryce Canyon Lodge 🖼 , *125–126, 139*
Bryce Canyon Lodge Restaurant ✕ , *138*
Bryce Canyon Lodge Gift Shop, *140*
Bryce Canyon National Park, *14, 116–154*
accessibility, *123*
admission fees, *34, 123*
books on, *26, 122*
camping, *149–150*
dining, *35, 124, 138–139, 145*
educational programs, *150–151*
emergencies, *27*
family fun, *25*
festivals, *44, 45*
flora and fauna, *139*
geology of, *129*
hiking, *25, 132, 134–135, 138, 142, 143–144, 151–152*
historic sites, *125–126*
history of, *125*
itineraries, *120–121*
lodging, *38–39, 123–124, 139, 146*
permits, *41*
picnic areas, *126, 141, 143*
price categories, *36, 124*
scenic drives, *127, 143, 145*
scenic stops, *127–129, 132, 141–142, 143*
shopping, *140, 146, 148*
sports and activities, *148–154*
top reasons to go, *116*
tours, *124–125, 146*
transportation, *119, 122*
visitor centers, *138*
visitor information, *125*
weather, *119*
Bryce Canyon Pines Campground and RV Park, *150*
Bryce Canyon Pines Motel 🖼 , *146*

Bryce Canyon Pines Restaurant ✕, *145*
Bryce Canyon Trading Post, *163*
Bryce Canyon Visitor Center, *138*
Bryce Canyon Winter Fest, *44*
Bryce Point, *127*
Bryce Wildlife Adventure, *145*
Bulloch's Drug Store ✕, *172*
Burger Barn ✕, *161*
Bus travel, *30, 32, 47, 54–55*

C

Cable Mountain Lodge 🖥, *98*
Calf Creek Falls Recreation Area, *180*
Camping
Bryce Canyon, *149–150*
Zion, *83–84*
Canyon Country Lodge 🖥, *183*
Canyon Overlook Trail, *21, 65*
Canyon Trail Rides, *87, 153*
Car travel and rentals, *32–33, 47, 55*
roadside emergencies, *33*
Castle Dome Café & Snack Bar ✕, *72*
Cedar Breaks Lodge 🖥, *165*
Cedar Breaks National Monument, *164–165*
Cedar City, UT, *157, 166, 169–174*
Cedar City Livestock & Heritage Festival, *46*
Centro Woodfired Pizzeria ✕, *170*
Checkerboard Mesa, *62, 64*
Chef Alfredo's Ristorante Italiano ✕, *170–171*
Christmas Bird Count, *46*

Church's Blue Pine Motel 🖥, *162*
Circle D Motel 🖥, *183*
Clark's Nutcracker, *16*
Cliffrose Springdale, Curie Collection 🖥, *98*
Cliffside Restaurant ✕, *107*
Climate, *43*
Coal Creek Trail, *173–174*
Cottonwood Meadow Lodge 🖥, *162–163*
Court of the Patriarchs, *64*
Covid-19, *28, 37–38*
Cowboy's Smokehouse Café ✕, *161*
Crawford Arch, *64*
Credit cards, *35*

D

David J. West Gallery, *99*
Deep Creek Coffee Company ✕, *97*
Desert Pearl Inn 🖥, *98*
Dining. ⇨ Also specific towns
Bryce Canyon, *35, 124, 138–139, 145*
Zion, *34–35, 58, 72*
Dixie National Forest, *169*
Dixie Roundup Rodeo, *45*
Driftwood Lodge 🖥, *98*

E

Educational programs
Bryce Canyon, *150–151*
Zion, *84–85*
Emerald Pools Trail, *21, 65*
Emergencies, *27*
Entrada Escalante Lodge 🖥, *183*
Entrada golf course, *113*
Erawan Thai ✕, *171*

Escalante, UT, *157, 175–177*
Escalante Canyons Art Festival, *45*
Escalante Outfitters, *176*
Escalante Outfitters Cabins 🖥, *183–184*
Escalante Outfitters Restaurant ✕, *181–182*
Escalante Petrified Forest State Park, *180*
Escape Goats, *176*
Excursions of Escalante, *177*
Expert Talks, *85*

F

Fairyland Loop Trail, *132*
Fairyland Point, *128*
Family fun, *25*
FeelLove Coffee ✕, *109*
Festival of the Americas, *44*
Festivals and seasonal events, *44–46*
Fishing, *85*
Flanigan's Inn 🖥, *99*
Flora and fauna, *16–19, 85*
4th West Pub, *184*
Foxes, *17*
French Spot, The ✕, *171*
Frontier Homestead State Park Museum, *169*
Full Moon Hike, *124*

G

Galaxy Diner and Motel ✕, *162*
Geology of the parks, *22, 129*
Geology Talks, *151*
George's Corner (bar), *111*
Georg's Ski Shop, *166*
Golf, *90, 101, 113*
Gooseberry Mesa, *101*

Grafton (ghost town), *94*
Great Basin Rattle-snake, *16*
Great White Throne, *64*
Grey Fox, *17*
Grotto picnic area, *62*
Grotto Trail, *86*

H

Hat Shop Trail, *142*
Health and safety, *28, 37–38*
Hell's Backbone Road, *180*
Hidden Canyon Trail, *68*
Highway *12 Scenic Byway, 180–181*
Hiking, *25*
 Bryce Canyon, 25, 132, 134–135, 138, 142, 143–144, 151–152
 Zion, 25, 64–65, 68, 70–71, 78–80, 86–87
Hole-in-the-Rock Road, *181*
Holiday Lights at Red Hills Desert Garden, *46*
Horseback riding
 Bryce Canyon, 152–153
 Zion, 87
Hurricane, UT, *90, 100–101*

I

IG Winery, *170*
Immunizations, *38*
Inn at Entrada, The 🏨 , *110*
Inn on the Cliff 🏨 , *110–111*
Inspiration Point, *128*
Internet access, *27*
Irmita's Casita ✕ , *107–108*
Iron Gate Inn 🏨 , *173*
Itineraries, *53*

K

Kayeneta Acoustic Roots Music for ALL Festival, *46*

Kayeneta Art Village, *102*
King's Landing Bis-tro ✕ , *96*
Kiva Koffeehouse ✕ , *182*
Kodachrome Basin State Park, *181*
Kolob Canyons and Kolob Terrace, *51, 73–81*
Kolob Canyons Road, *74*
Kolob Canyons View-point, *74, 76*
Kolob Canyons Visitor Center, *81*
Kolob Terrace Road, *74, 76*

L

La Verkin Creek Trail, *78–79*
Lava Point, *76*
Lava Point Camp-ground, *83–84*
Ledges Golf Course, *113*
Lee Pass, *78*
Lizards, *17*
Lodging. ⇨ **Also spe-cific towns**
 Bryce Canyon, 38–39, 123–124, 139, 146
 Zion, 38–39, 57–58, 73

M

Main Park Road, *127*
Main Street Café ✕ , *100–101*
Mammals, *16–17*
Maynard Dixon Living History Museum and Gallery, *113–114*
Milt's Stage Stop ✕ , *171*
Morty's Cafe ✕ , *108*
Mossy Cave, *128*
Mossy Cave Trail, *132*
Mountain Ridge Cab-ins 🏨 , *163*
Mt. Carmel Junction, UT, *90, 113–114*

N

Narrows Trail, *21, 68*
Native Americans, *135*
Natural Bridge, *141*
Navajo Loop Trail, *20, 132*
Navajo Trail/Queen's Garden Combination Loop, *134*
North Campground, *149–150*
North Campground Picnic Area, *126*
North Campground Viewpoint, *129*
North Creek Left Fork Trail, *78*

O

Observation Point, *68, 70*
Orderville Canyon Trail, *70*
Oscar's Café ✕ , *96*

P

Packing, *40*
Painted Pony ✕ , *108*
Paiute people, *22*
Panguitch, UT, *156, 160–163*
Panguitch Lake Ice Fishing Derby, *44*
Panguitch Valley Balloon Rally, *45*
Paria View, *141–142*
Park House Cafe ✕ , *96–97*
Pa'rus Trail, *21, 70*
Passports, *40*
Pastry Pub ✕ , *171–172*
Peekaboo Loop, *21, 134*
Peregrine Falcon, *16*
Permits, *40–41, 57*
Picnic areas
 Bryce Canyon, 126
 Zion, 62, 74
Piracy Point, *142*
PorkBelly's Eatery ✕ , *172*
Prairie dogs, *16, 152*

Price categories
Bryce Canyon dining, 36, 124
Bryce Canyon lodging, 39, 124
Zion dining, 36, 58
Zion lodging, 39, 58
Pronghorn Antelope, *17*

Q

Quality Inn Zion 🏨 , *101*
Queen's Garden Trail, *20, 134–135*
Quilt Walk Festival, *45*

R

Rainbow Point, *116, 143*
Ranger programs, *25*
Bryce Canyon, 150–151
Zion, 84–85
Red Canyon, *161*
Red Cliffs Desert Garden, *104–105*
Red Cliffs Desert Reserve, *104*
Red Mountain Resort 🏨 , *111*
Red Rock Grill at Zion Lodge ✕ , *72*
Reptiles, *16–17*
Riggs Spring Loop Trail, *144*
Rim Trail, *20, 135*
Rim Walk, *125*
Riverside Walk, *70*
Rock climbing, *87–88*
Rowley's Red Barn, *112*
Ruby's General Store, *146, 148*
Ruby's Guided ATV Tours, *125*
Ruby's Horseback Adventures, *53*
Ruby's Inn Campground and RV Park, *150*
Ruby's Inn Mountain Bike Rentals, *149*
Ruby's Winter Activities Center, *154*
Rusty's Ranch House ✕ , *172*

S

St. George, UT, *90, 101–113*
St. George Art Festival, *44*
St. George Art Museum, *105*
St. George Children's Museum, *105*
St. George Dinosaur Discovery Site at Johnson Farm, *105–106*
St. George StreetFest, *44*
St. George Tabernacle, *106*
St. George Temple, *106*
Scarecrow Walk and Haunted Canyon, *46*
Scenic Byway *12, 127*
Serenidad Gallery, *184*
700 Degree Artisan Pizza ✕ , *108*
Shopping
Bryce Canyon, 140, 146, 148
Zion, 73
Skiing
Brian Head, 166
Bryce Canyon, 154
Zion, 88
Sky Mountain Golf Course, *101*
Slot Canyons Inn B&B 🏨 , *184*
Smoking, *36*
Snakes, *16*
Snow Canyon State Park, *105*
Snowshoeing, *88, 154, 166*
Sol Foods Supermarket, *99*
South Campground, *84*
Southern Utah Museum of Art, *170*
Springdale, UT, *90*
Spotted Dog Café ✕ , *97*
Stone Canyon Inn 🏨 , *174–175*
Stone Hearth Grille ✕ , *174*

Subway Bottoms-Up Trail, *79*
Subway Top-Down Trail, *79–80*
Sunrise Point, *129, 131*
Sunset Campground, *150*
Swimming, *25, 88*

T

Tandoori Taqueria ✕ , *162*
Taxes, *41*
Taylor Creek Trail, *80*
Telescopes Program, *151*
Timber Creek Overlook Trail, *80*
Tipping, *41, 42*
Tower Bridge Trail, *138*
Train travel, *33, 47*
Transportation, *30, 32–33, 47*
Tropic, *157, 174–175*
Tuacahn amphitheater, *111*
TwentyFive Main Cafe ✕ , *108–109*

U

U.S. *89/Utah's Heritage Highway, 145*
Under-the-Rim Trail, *116, 141–142*
Urban Renewal (shop), *112*
Utah Canyon Outdoors, *177*
Utah Midsummer Renaissance Faire, *45*
Utah Prairie Dog, *16*
Utah Shakespearean Festival, *45, 169*

V

Valhalla Pizzeria & Coffee Shop ✕ , *138–139*
Visa, *41*
Visitor Center Bookstore, *140*

Visitor centers
Bryce Canyon, 138
Zion, 71, 81

W

Walking tours, 124–125
Watchman Trail, 70–71
Water Ouzel, 17
Weather, 43
Weeping Rock, 64
Weeping Rock Trail, 71
West Rim Trail, 80
When to go, 41, 43
Whiptail Lizard, 17
Whiteman Bench, 141
Wild Turkey, 17
Wood Ash Rye ✕ , 109
Worthington Gallery, 99–100

X

Xetava Garden Cafe
✕ , 109

Y

Yovimpa Point, 116, 143

Z

Zion Adventure Company, 81
Zion Brewery Station II Bar, 111
Zion Canyon, 51, 59–65, 68, 70–73
Zion Canyon Brew Pub, 99

Zion Canyon Visitor Center, 71
Zion Canyon Visitor Center Store, 73
Zion Cycles, 82
Zion Gateways, 14, 90–114
dining, 93, 96–97, 100–101, 107–109
Hurricane, 90, 100–101
lodging, 98–99, 101, 110–111, 114
Mount Carmel Junction, 90, 113–114
nightlife and the arts, 99, 111
price categories, 93
St. George, 90, 101–113
shopping, 99–100, 112
sports and activities, 101, 112–113
Springdale, 90, 93–100
top reasons to go, 90
transportation, 94
Zion Guru, 81
Zion Human History Museum, 60
Zion Lodge ⛺ , 60, 73
Zion Lodge Gift Shop, 73
Zion Narrows Trail, 21
Zion National Park, 14, 50–88
admission fees, 34, 57
books on, 26, 57
camping, 83–84
climate, 54
dining, 34–35, 58, 72
educational programs, 84–85

emergencies, 27
family fun, 25
festivals, 44–46
flora and fauna, 85
geological landmarks, 60
hiking, 25, 64–65, 68, 70–71, 78–80
historic sites, 60
history of, 23–24
itineraries, 53
Kolob Canyons and Kolob Terrace, 51, 73–81
lodging, 38–39, 57–58, 73
permits, 40–41, 57
picnic areas, 62, 74
price categories, 36, 58
scenic drives, 62, 74, 76
scenic stops, 62, 64, 76
shopping, 73
sports and activities, 81–83, 85–88
top reasons to go, 50–51
tours, 58–59, 81
transportation, 54–56
visitor centers, 71, 81
visitor information, 59
when to go, 54
Zion National Park Forever Project, 84
Zion Pizza & Noodle Co. ✕ , 97
Zion Ponderosa Ranch Resort ⛺ , 114
Zion Rock and Mountain Guides, 87–88

Photo Credits

Fodor's InFocus ZION & BRYCE CANYON NATIONAL PARKS

Publisher: Stephen Horowitz, *General Manager*

Editorial: Douglas Stallings, *Editorial Director;* Jill Fergus, Jacinta O'Halloran, Amanda Sadlowski, *Senior Editors;* Kayla Becker, Alexis Kelly, *Editors*

Design: Tina Malaney, *Design and Production Director;* Jessica Gonzalez, *Graphic Designer;* Mariana Tabares, *Design and Production Intern*

Production: Jennifer DePrima, *Editorial Production Manager;* Elyse Rozelle, *Senior Production Editor;* Monica White, *Production Editor*

Maps: Rebecca Baer, *Senior Map Editor;* Mark Stroud (Moon Street Cartography), *Cartographer*

Photography: Viviane Teles, *Senior Photo Editor;* Namrata Aggarwal, Ashok Kumar, Carl Yu, *Photo Editors;* Rebecca Rimmer, *Photo Intern*

Business and Operations: Chuck Hoover, *Chief Marketing Officer;* Robert Ames, *Group General Manager;* Devin Duckworth, *Director of Print Publishing;* Victor Bernal, *Business Analyst*

Public Relations and Marketing: Joe Ewaskiw, *Senior Director Communications and Public Relations*

Fodors.com: Jeremy Tarr, *Editorial Director;* Rachael Levitt, *Managing Editor*

Technology: Jon Atkinson, *Director of Technology;* Rudresh Teotia, *Lead Developer;* Jacob Ashpis, *Content Operations Manager*

Writer: Shelly Arenas

Editor: Laura M. Kidder

Production Editor: Jennifer DePrima

2nd Edition

ISBN 978-1-64097-450-0

ISSN 1946-309X

All details in this book are based on information supplied to us at press time. Always confirm information when it matters, especially if you're making a detour to visit a specific place. Fodor's expressly disclaims any liability, loss, or risk, personal or otherwise, that is incurred as a consequence of the use of any of the contents of this book.

SPECIAL SALES

This book is available at special discounts for bulk purchases for sales promotions or premiums. For more information, e-mail SpecialMarkets@fodors.com.

PRINTED IN CANADA

10 9 8 7 6 5 4 3 2 1

About Our Writer

 Shelley Arenas has been a regular contributor to Fodor's for nearly two decades, sharing her knowledge of and love for the western United States and its national parks. A native of Washington State, she has covered eastern Washington and the state's three national parks for Fodor's *Pacific Northwest* and Fodor's *The Complete Guide to the National Parks of the West*. She updated the Zion, Bryce Canyon, and Capitol Reef national parks chapters in the most recent edition of Fodor's *Utah*. For this book, she loved exploring southern Utah in more depth to further reveal for readers the wonders of the Zion/Bryce Canyon region and the myriad ways to enjoy them.